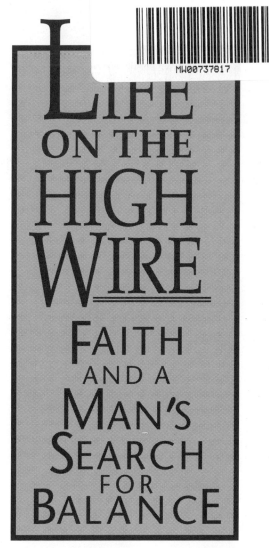

# LIFE
## ON THE
# HIGH
# WIRE

## FAITH
### AND A
## MAN'S
## SEARCH
### FOR
## BALANCE

# MARTIN CAMP

**DIMENSIONS**
FOR LIVING

LIFE ON THE HIGH WIRE:
Faith and a Man's Search for Balance

*This book is printed on recycled, acid-free paper.*

**Library of Congress Cataloging-in-Publication Data**

Camp, Martin, 1954–
    Life on the high wire  :  faith and a man's search for balance / Martin Camp.
        p.  cm.
    **ISBN 0-687-05239-4** (alk. paper)
    1. Men—Religious life.   2. Christian life.   I. Title.
    BV4843.C36   1997
    248.8'42—dc21                                                                           96-39503

Scripture quotations are taken from the New Revised Standard Version Bible, Copyright 1989 by the Division of Christian Education of the National Council of the Churches of Christ in the USA. Used by permission.

97 98 99 00 01 02 03 04 05 06—10 9 8 7 6 5 4 3 2 1

MANUFACTURED IN THE UNITED STATES OF AMERICA

I want to dedicate this book to my father, my wife, and my three children. Who I am and all I have learned about life is intertwined in my relationships with these wonderful people, my family. They provide the foundation, the balance in my life.

My father, Cameron J. Camp, Jr., showed me by his life what it means to survive, to overcome, to keep going when the tough times come. My wife of nineteen years, Kay Grammer Camp, has been a rock of support for me throughout all the challenges life has thrown our way. Knowing she is there, beside me, has given me the strength to persevere. My three children, Eric, Leigh, and Haydon, have taught me what it means to be a father—the joy and pain of parenting. Their enthusiasm, humor, and constant love have completed the circle of life for me. I can see myself in my children and understand more fully my father and what he experienced raising me.

To the extent I ever achieve the life well lived, it will be lived in the love of this family—God's most precious gifts to me on earth.

# CONTENTS

Preface . . . . . . . . . . . . . . . . . . . . . . . . . . . . . . . . . . . . . . . . . . . . . . . 9

The Drive for Excellence and the Balanced Life

1. Why Not the Best? . . . . . . . . . . . . . . . . . . . . . . . . . . . . . . . . . 13
   (Understanding What "My Best" Means in Life's Many Roles)

2. Too Large a Pizza Pan and Too Little Dough!. . . . . . . . . . . . 19
   (Learning to Live with Limits)

3. Crossroads . . . . . . . . . . . . . . . . . . . . . . . . . . . . . . . . . . . . . . . 24
   (Avoiding the "Slippery Slope" by Making Right Decisions)

4. Why Go to Church? . . . . . . . . . . . . . . . . . . . . . . . . . . . . . . . . 29
   (Discovering What Church Is All About)

What Does It Mean to Be a Man?

5. What Separates the Men from the Boys?. . . . . . . . . . . . . . . 36
   (Unpacking the Media's Image of a Man)

6. I'm Only Human . . . ? . . . . . . . . . . . . . . . . . . . . . . . . . . . . . 41
   (Accepting Responsibility Instead of Looking for Scapegoats)

7. On Our Own Special Course Through Time. . . . . . . . . . . . 45
   (Aging, and How to Avoid Being Unbalanced by Others)

8. How Deep Is Your Rudder?. . . . . . . . . . . . . . . . . . . . . . . . . . 52
   (Keeping Your Balance Against the Prevailing Winds)

## A Man and His Work

9. Have You Put God in a Box?........................57
(Making Room for God in Your Work)

10. Does God Care About My Work?.....................62
(Asking Tough Questions When the Sacrifice Doesn't Seem Worth It)

11. The Myth of the Perfect Job........................68
(Setting Realistic Expectations)

## He Who Dies with the Most Toys—Dies!

12. Daily Bread........................................74
(Determining How Much Is Enough)

13. What Do Men Live By? ............................78
(Meeting Others' Needs)

14. What Will They Say About Me When I'm Gone?.........82
(Reflecting on the Life Well-Lived)

## Fathers and Sons

15. Whose Life Am I Living?............................87
(Becoming Your Own Man)

16. My Dad Is a Workaholic............................92
(Taking Charge of Your Life)

17. My Father, My Friend...............................98
(Seeing Yourself in the Eyes of Your Father)

## A Friend in Need

18. Knowledge Is Power...............................103
(Recognizing Your Need for Friends and Intimacy)

19. He Was My Age, and He Was Dying..................109
(Staying Involved Through the Pain)

20. When a Friend Is Hurting .........................115
(Being a Friend in Difficult Times)

21. One True Love .................................... 119
    (Overcoming the Myth of the "Perfect" Mate)

22. My Friend Peter Pan ............................. 125
    (Choosing Commitment)

Acceptance and Grace

23. The Power of an Imperfect Life ...................... 131
    (Letting Go of "Happily Ever After" Expectations)

24. The Peculiar Contentment of the Christian Life ........ 136
    (Finding Real Joy)

25. Is My Life Too Complicated? ........................ 140
    (Offering Your Life as a Gift to God)

Epilogue ............................................ 145

Questions for Reflection or Discussion ................... 147

# PREFACE

This book is written by a man for men. This is not to say that women would not enjoy reading it. In fact, I hope many women will read this book, if only to better understand the men in their lives—fathers, husbands, sons, brothers, and friends. But my primary reason for writing this book is to open a dialogue with other men about what it means to be a man—a Christian man—in this time. This book is not about beating drums or blaming parents or looking at the biological or astrological differences between men and women. I will let others do that. This book is about issues common to all men who are trying to achieve excellence and balance in a world of unrealistic expectations.

The urgency for this book grew out of an experience I had a few years ago on a ten-mile run. I had set out on a course that circles around a lake. About five miles out, it started to rain—not a warm, gentle rain that would lift my spirits. No, this was a hard, bone-chilling rain. It turned the dirt track into a mud slick and exhausted me. I felt almost overcome against the powerful forces of nature. There was no sense in turning back, because there would be five grueling miles of torture in either direction. There was no place to wait it out; and even if I did find shelter, there was no way to know how long the storm would last. I pressed on, determined to stick it out.

As I ran, and the rain continued to beat down on me, I had truly had it: frustrated at the weather that ruined my run, angry at myself for not paying more attention to the black clouds that had seemed so far away when I started, uneasy when I found the trail blocked by construction and had to detour along the riverbank, and downright scared when I slipped and almost fell down the embankment into the rushing water below.

I resigned myself to suffering through the remaining miles, sustained by the hope of a hot shower. It occurred to me that this run, this experience of being "beat up" with no choice other than to continue, was exactly the way I felt about my life—about all the responsibilities I faced each day.

Every day was a matter of survival. I was so busy with the struggle that I could think of nothing but getting through each day's agenda. In almost every area of my life, particularly at work, there seemed to be no opportunity to turn back and no shelter from a storm of pressures. There was only responsibility, and the frustration, anger, and sense of being put upon by forces outside myself.

As I ran, I knew that there were other men who felt the same way, so I wondered how they coped. I also wondered how my faith was supposed to fit into this struggle. In my mind's eye, I could see a group of men meeting regularly to discuss these issues and share their insights. When I returned to my office, I wrote letters to several friends. We started meeting, and our group began to grow. I found that there is strength in meeting with others and talking through these issues. There was the feeling of being a team, being united in a common purpose. It overcame the loneliness that often hits us when we are unguarded. Many of the chapters in this book grew out of those meetings.

This book is written for any man who has ever felt overwhelmed by all the tasks he has been told he must do in today's overprogrammed world. It is written for the man who wonders how his faith is related to the real world of living and working today, in these times. It is written for the man who wants to explore the role of values and principles in bringing some order to this chaos—not to eliminate the conflicts, for they cannot be eliminated—but to find the peace to accept them and the joy to laugh when that is the best he can do. It is written for the man who feels that everyone seems to be on the same treadmill at some sports club, where the coach keeps increasing the speed. This intense pressure to excel in all areas of our lives at the same time is just too much.

This is one Christian's attempt to understand this struggle in the context of how we are called to live our lives as followers of Christ. It is an attempt to see the connections between the values we are taught in our churches and the daily crises we must face twenty-four hours a day, seven days a week.

What are my "qualifications" for writing this book? I am a husband, a father, a son, a brother, a friend, a working man with too much to do and not enough time, a churchgoer and volunteer, a member of too many groups wanting too much time, a storyteller, and a sometimes teacher. Like other men, I am struggling to juggle it all. Like other men, I make mistakes, drop the ball, do stupid things, ask for undeserved forgiveness, and am grateful when I receive it. My experiences are not unique. I believe other men will see bits and pieces of their lives in these pages. We all feel that we are running in the storm of life together. We all want to regain the moral high ground, to find a new sense of balance in an imbalanced world.

Martin Camp

# 1

# WHY NOT THE BEST?

## UNDERSTANDING WHAT "MY BEST" MEANS IN LIFE'S MANY ROLES

*"They [the scribes and Pharisees] do all their deeds to be seen by others; for they make their phylacteries broad and their fringes long. They love to have the place of honor at banquets and the best seats in the synagogues."*

Matthew 23:5-6

President Carter wrote a book titled *Why Not the Best?* I must admit I have not read it. However, I have always wondered where this preoccupation with "the best" comes from. The best schools for our kids, the best job, the best house, the best neighborhood, the best lawn, the best movie, the best restaurant, the best sports team, the best country, the best church—the list goes on and on. We are barraged with books and lists of who's who. We hear about the best mechanic, the best athlete, the best actor, the best of anything.

I was recently reminded of how deeply I am infected with this disease. I had planned a special getaway with my wife, Kay, at a river resort. I had even gone there ahead of time to check it out. This was going to be a winner! Based upon the knowledge I had gathered from my scouting trip and a map I brought home for further study, I had reserved the stone cottage I knew would have the "best" view of the river. When we arrived on Friday night, it was too dark to see much. The next morning, however, I eagerly looked out the window for what I was sure was going to be an outstanding view of the river. I could see it, all right. But I had to strain to do it! I had to look around the roofs of two other cottages situated below the balcony of my carefully selected retreat. I was chagrined and disappointed. The cabin was fine, but it lacked something. It did not have the "best" view!

Later that morning I confided my disappointment to Kay.

She laughed and said, "It may not have the best view, but it has a good view, and besides, look how little yard those two cottages below us have, how close they are to the road, how much less private they are. I'm happy with the cabin you chose. It is the best, as far as I'm concerned." She had to be the best wife a guy could have! She seemed sincere, and her logic was consistent. I was impressed by her sense of balance. Here was a situation in which I had lost my perspective, my feeling for a balanced viewpoint. Somehow, however, she had brought me back to equilibrium.

Let's face it—there is nothing wrong with the concept of wanting the best. The Bible certainly speaks of giving God our very best; the fatted calf, the sacrifice without blemish, the first (the best) fruits of harvest. It also reports that Jesus made distinctions. He saw one thing as better than another. When Martha goes ahead with the chores, and her sister, Mary, holds back and listens to Jesus, Martha criticizes Mary. She left her to do all the work! Jesus, however, makes a different kind of distinction. He asserts that Mary has made the better choice.

So why am I so driven about this business of being the best? Why do I feel that something is out of whack about it? Is it a fear of failure, of what happens if I'm not my best? Maybe. I don't want to get too psychological, but I'm sure it could also reflect a resentment at trying to meet what I perceive as someone else's program for my life, someone else's ideas of my best.

We've all been caught up in this. There is a fine line between having high expectations and being driven by someone else's unrealistic demands. Someone may have meant no harm, but unrealistic demands hurt. They pinch the soul. They burden our lives. I have been there. So have you. Pretty soon you fear that you won't measure up. Failure—the very word sends shivers of pain up my spine. What could be worse than any kind of failure in a society focused on the best?

As a child, I knew that my parents had high expectations of me. They made sure that I knew it. One look at my aptitude test scores, and I was expected to make straight A's. After all, my older brother and sister did! That made it unbearable. Could they not understand that I was different? What my brother and sister felt about all this, I never knew. But I hated this pressure. And I hated feeling alone, feeling that no one really understood.

I want you to know that this was not your ordinary, garden variety, down-to-earth view of excellence. It was a painfully rigid kind of excellence, a mom asking what questions you missed, since you had only made a 98, not a 100. It was a father who would take out his belt if you missed too many spelling words in a practice drill at home. I remember when my older brother came in second in a speech contest in high school.

My mom's only response: "If you had practiced as much as Patrick, you would have won." Never mind that Patrick was a National Merit finalist, with raw talent far surpassing the others in his class. Never mind at all that my brother had practiced, had tried to do an outstanding job. Second was not the best.

The B's and, heaven forbid, the occasional C's I made in elementary school fell down like an iron curtain between me and the two older perfect students. My parents, much to their dismay, did not know what to make of me. I can remember the pain of hearing the front-seat parents discussing "What's wrong with Martin?" as I sat in the back, being driven home from school with a report card that, in their eyes, did not reflect the "best" I could do. I felt a sense of imbalance, a loss of some inner center.

Why do such things haunt us still? One reason is that when our children come along, the same attitudes reappear in us, like germs that have been dormant for years. I know this from personal experience. Now in the middle of my life, I am the father of three highly gifted kids. Certainly I want the best for them. Who wouldn't? But—here it comes—I also want them to do their best!

I remember when my oldest son, Eric, was a sixth grader. He was a great kid. I should have thanked God every day. Then he brought home his first C on the six-week report card, a 79 in math. Barely a C, but nevertheless a C. He was in the honors math program yet! On the standardized tests, he always scored near the top for students his age. The raw ability was there, and doing well in school had always come easy for him. Obviously, from my perspective, a 79 was not his best.

I decided I needed to spend some quality, one-on-one time with my son, to discuss this grade and, more to the point, to fix whatever problem had caused it. We went to an Italian restaurant, one of his favorites, just the two of us. We talked about the 79. My son explained, at first, that since he was so smart, so gifted and talented in math, the 79 merely reflected a teacher who couldn't teach. Clever, but I didn't buy that. We went further into it. We then analyzed what had gone wrong with a big project in the course, one on which he had made a 75, which had been the primary grade for the six-week period. To ask him, it should have gotten a high grade.

Only a few items remained. He had done the report in pencil, not pen. His teacher counted off 5 points. He had not cited his source—another 5 points off. She had disagreed with some of his statements that, in the original Roman numeral system, 4 was IIII, not IV—his cleverest idea—and that the concept of place was not part of the system, so that the original sequence of lettering didn't matter. She had written, "I don't think so," and took off another 15 points. Eric had argued back, claiming that the author of his source book, Isaac Asimov, certainly knew more than his teacher, so he (and Isaac Asimov) were right and she was wrong. Of course, since he didn't have his source, having turned it back in to the public library, he was not able to prove to her the facts in his report.

We talked some more. I said that being smart isn't enough, that you need to work hard and also figure out what is expected. It doesn't matter, I told him, if you just *know* the material. There is more to it than that. If you don't play by the teacher's rules, you won't get the top grade.

Obviously, I felt that I had done an outstanding job—the best—at a father-son talk. I was proud of myself, glad we had had such a good heart-to-heart talk, proud of what a great dad I was—so sensitive, caring, a real nineties guy. My son wasn't fooled for a second.

The next day he told his mom, "Boy, there sure is a big difference around here between a 79 and an 80." His best had almost been a B, but I had been so wrapped up in correcting him that I had missed that. I had lost balance without realizing it.

Personally, there is not a thing wrong with this concept of best. On the level of principle, the realm of the ideal, it is even admirable. Who wouldn't agree? But when I begin to apply it in the microcosm of my day-to-day life—big troubles appear. Being the best in one area often interferes with being the best in other areas. If I isolate each area in its proper place, I can define the best course of action: what I think the best lawyer would do in a given situation, or the best father, the best husband, son, or friend. But how do you reconcile the conflict when one or more of these bests wreak havoc in some other area? What can you do when your "bests" collide? Would the best lawyer cancel the weekend trip with the family to close the deal for his client, or would the best husband tell the client that business would have to wait?

It comes down to this: Are we going to be defeated by this principle of doing the best? Do we just neglect it and all those who planted it in our minds? Or can we do something creative with it? I think the answer may lie in taking a new look at this concept of the best. We can benefit from it, make it work for us, and enjoy it. However, we can't leave it like it is.

We can begin by redefining it. Take it apart. Put some realistic limits into it. I'll tell you what I discovered. You can make it into something very useful. It will do a lot for you. But this won't be easy. I discovered that I need to put some effort into my own life, to rediscover and to realign some things. I need to take time, like the weekend escape with my wife, in places that lend themselves to contemplative moments, even if I don't have the cottage with the best view.

You put some time into this, and you may discover what I did—that in Christ, I am called to love and accept my limits, to temper my failures, to judge myself not just by others' expectations, but more profoundly, in the charity of a God who welcomes the prodigal son back with a fattened calf. Surely this God of mercy and redemption can forgive 98's instead of 100's, and mistaken choices in time spent at work or at home. Yes, we can strive for the best, and when we work at this in a new way, we can begin to integrate it into our total experience in a very powerful and helpful way. In fact, it actually can add to our sense of personal balance.

# 2

# TOO LARGE A PIZZA PAN AND TOO LITTLE DOUGH!

## LEARNING TO LIVE WITH LIMITS

*For everything there is a season, and a time
for every matter under heaven.*

Ecclesiastes 3:1

**M**y experience with "success" or "motivational" seminars is that the first half of the day is spent pumping the participants up with tale after tale of people who have achieved excellence in their chosen endeavors. There are stories about Bruce Jenner, who after he lost his first Olympic Decathlon, wrote out the scores he would achieve in the next Olympics and focused so intently on those scores that he achieved each one, winning the gold medal four years later. Another favorite example is Wilma Rudolph, who overcame childhood polio to become the fastest woman of her time, defying doctors who insisted she would always need braces.

There are countless rags to riches stories that certainly inspire. But let's face it: Who can do such things? And even if we could, would we really want to shape our lives that way? It has always struck me that many of those people who achieve such rare excellence seem one-dimensional, out of balance. How can there be balance in a life so devoted to accomplishing one thing?

Somewhere in the second half of the success seminar, the speaker often passes out a questionnaire concerning how you spend your time. What are you doing in your career, your community, your church? How much time do you devote to your family and friends, and to yourself? Your answers are then converted into numerical equivalents and plotted on a graph. The resulting picture is supposed to represent your life. If the geometric figure is a circle, you are then well-rounded. You supposedly are free to roll smoothly down the road of a balanced life. On the other hand, if the figure is irregular in shape, as is more often the case, you are out of balance. This means that you devote entirely too much time to one or two facets of your life. Never mind that most of us have this pattern. You are considered out-of-joint. But there is more.

Here is where they begin to drop the ball. They give great examples of these people with one-dimensional commitments to excel, but then they urge you to become well-rounded. At what cost? More than one basic incongruity exists here. How can you give all your efforts in a single focus of energy to be a "winner," like one of those incredible heroes mentioned in the morning session, and still be "well-rounded"?

Running out there in the rain that day, I began to collapse inside. I was overwhelmed. Burnout was close at hand. How could I possibly be the best father, husband, lawyer, churchman, community volunteer that I could possibly be with the talents I have been given, while simultaneously trying to take care of myself physically and mentally? And how, while trying to do all these worthwhile things, could I also attempt to be "well-rounded"? I felt exactly like a baker in a pizza shop who is told to make an extra large pizza, but is given only enough dough for a small one. As I stretch the "dough" to the outer rim of the pan in one area of my life, something snaps in another area. A hole appears. And as I stretch the dough to patch the hole, the original side snaps back.

Do you recall Lucille Ball in the famous "I Love Lucy" episode in the runaway candy factory? She and Ethel can't shut off the conveyor belt, so they frantically begin to stuff candy into their mouths and clothes. When this happens to me, I feel that everything is out of control. I am overwhelmed by the tasks in front of me, unable to stop the machine or cope with the volume of output required.

I want to reject this dilemma of the crazy pizza baker because its view of excellence and balance is based upon a false premise. I have found that I cannot be excellent in all areas of my life simultaneously. And I cannot please everyone, including myself, all the time. I simply cannot live up to this unachievable combination of excellence and balance. It, and I along with it, were doomed from the start. Once when the energy required to carry on this struggle was too great, I joked to some overachiever friends that I would write my own self-help book. I would call it *Dare to Be Average!* How can any of us really try our best at anything and find a sense of balance?

Is there another option? Are the only two avenues that of impossible pizza baking or of giving up? It has not been easy, but I have discovered another choice. Reading the book of Ecclesiastes, I found it full of wisdom about time and the struggle for excellence. It provides an interesting perspective. There truly is "nothing new under the sun."

What this conveyed to me is that we have always struggled with balance. Yet ironically, this struggle may have intensified in the Western nations. It is a paradox, but our very technology and affluence have backfired. They have freed us from many of the physical restraints that forced patterns, rhythms, into the lives of earlier, simpler generations. These rhythms provided a sense of measure and an assurance of order.

But the pressures of life today are entirely different. The incredible drive toward survival in our work, the emphasis on achievement, and the ideal goal of success in more areas are ultimately destructive for many of us. There are specific reasons for sometimes feeling that you are about to come unglued. This drive toward excellence is no help. In some ways, it is our worst enemy.

The old traditional wisdom of Ecclesiastes, on the other hand, can be our friend. It tells us that there really is a time for everything, a rhythm to life. Recognition of this rhythm, this ebb and flow, is the key to the whole thing. It came to me that I could reinterpret this sense of rhythm. I could find it again in my own life. It would involve a moment-by-moment struggle of prioritizing, evaluating, and reprioritizing. But I was determined to make it work. I would take a new look at the way I spend my time and energy. I would also accept some new limits in my life. I would, whether anybody liked it or not, accept the reality that I could not be two places at the same time. I was through trying to be Superman. I just wanted to be me, the best me that I could become without tearing that pizza.

Once I rejected the pizza-pan image, I needed a new goal and a new symbol to represent it. As I pondered this balancing process, in the context of recognizing that there is a time and season for everything, I remembered a consumer product we once purchased when I was a child. It was called Dial-A-Flavor and consisted of a circular canister divided into wedge-shaped compartments, with a spigot at the top. This spigot could be rotated from compartment to compartment, allowing the holder to shake out different flavored powders to create chocolate-, banana-, or strawberry-flavored milk. The Dial-A-Flavor idea seemed to hold real possibilities. After all, it focused on only one flavor at a time. It could be chocolate or strawberry or banana, but it couldn't be all three.

My life could be better lived as a giant Dial-A-Flavor canister. It is, in fact, divided into sections. At best, I am limited to focusing on one or two at a time. I cannot be at the office and at my son's baseball game at the same time, nor can I be at dinner with my wife and at a church meeting simultaneously. The image suggested this: The secret may be to keep a close watch on the amount of "flavor powder"—that is, time and energy—in each compartment, each area of my life. When I am working in any area, I must shake the "canister" as hard as I can and focus most of my energies on getting that particular job done right. But before all the powder is used up, I need to rotate the spigot, concentrate on another area, and let the first compartment be refilled. This image definitely had possibilities.

On the other hand, this Dial-A-Flavor analogy does not deny the struggle for balance. In fact, it helps to support the struggle, confirming that each day the "spigot" must be switched. Each day, each activity requires evaluation, choice, and fresh commitment. It gives a new meaning to the word *prioritize*. It also helps me to recognize that no human talent is limitless. I am definitely limited. So are you. Because we are limited, we need to struggle daily in the use of our time. I also find that a daily Serenity Prayer provides much strength in this struggle. Continually seeking the acceptance of things I cannot change, the courage to change things I can, and the wisdom to know the difference—this acknowledges my need for help and guidance from God. I try to remember that even Christ had to take time to restore himself, to escape to the desert.

I also have resolved to let someone else bake the pizza!

# 3

# CROSSROADS

## AVOIDING THE "SLIPPERY SLOPE" BY MAKING RIGHT DECISIONS

*"Enter through the narrow gate; for the gate is wide and the way is easy that leads to destruction, and there are many who take it. For the gate is narrow and the way is hard that leads to life, and there are few who find it."*

Matthew 7:13-14

"T he Road Not Taken" by Robert Frost is one of my favorite poems. As I read through its lines, I can see in Frost's "yellow wood" the two paths leading in different directions, a man poised at the beginning, trying to decide which way to go. The situation demands that he choose, because he would be unlikely to take the untraveled, the unchosen path.

I thought of this poem when we were on vacation a few years ago. We stayed in a small house, an old homestead in the little community of Leakey, Texas. The cabin was nestled beside the Frio River, surrounded by acres of grass and ancient pecan trees. It was decorated with handsome antique furniture, hardwood floors, metal ceilings, and ceiling fans. There was no television, no telephone, no air conditioning. The weather was unseasonably cool, and the river was downright cold. It was a Norman Rockwell scene: my wife, our three children, a friend for our then eleven-year-old to play with; cooking outside over the open fire in cast-iron skillets on a brick barbecue pit; croquet, horseshoes, board games, cards; a side road off the beaten path, a moment's respite from the fast lane.

24

I was called to a client crisis only once during the week—one jarring moment when the tranquility of the scene was interrupted as I stood at a pay phone next to the highway, being a lawyer once more.

The very act of coming to that area had demanded a choice. We could have gone elsewhere. I thought then of "The Road Not Taken," and of the specific decision to come to Leakey and the Frio River, a different world from our normal urban environment. I had decided to take a different path, and I, along with my wife, had chosen it for our entire family.

That was not the only time I had thought about crossroads on that trip. The second time occurred as I was going through an antique dresser in the cabin and discovered several old books. Of all things, one that caught my eye was a 1956 copy of *The Discipline of the Methodist Church.* I idly turned its pages. As I read the pronouncements of the church, the fears and concerns of the people, their attempt to respond with integrity to the problems of the world, I thought that we were actually much like them. They had great challenges. Their language spoke of the problems of broken homes, divorce, poverty, inadequate housing. They were worried about a world on the brink of nuclear war.

The map, describing the various countries where their denomination was established, showed vast areas where the reign of communism prevented delegates from attending the world conferences. In their official resolutions, they declared that they, as a people of God, were at the crossroads, that the decisions they made would have an impact on the world. They seemed to feel that God had given them a special responsibility, more than any other previous generation, to set the course of the future. There was a profound sense of balance about their lives. I was drawn to a page that seemed to capture the spirit of those people:

*Only Christlike people working under the empowerment and direction of a Christlike God can create and sustain a world which can long exist in this atomic era. Let it be understood, events of this turbulent time will*

25

*not wait patiently for our convenience. The world has been in the forge of
great travail. It now is upon the anvil, flaming hot, it is soft and mal-
leable. Almost anything can be made of it from paradise beyond our
dreams to hell more hideous than our worst fears. For a few fleeting years
we are the man at the anvil. Soon the metal will harden and what we
have made, we have made. . . . We who wish to be known as friends of
Jesus Christ have our chance now. The Church has arrived at the hour of
unsurpassed opportunity. If we believe in Him and will serve Him, the
time is now! "Behold now is the accepted time; behold, now is the day of
salvation."*

Those were powerful words, whether you agreed with all of
them or not. I was impressed by the spirit of such a people, with
their poise and command of the language, with the depth of their
concern and their ability to articulate it. But even more, I was
impressed by the similarity of our situations. We often hear the
same language used in churches about our generation, about the
crossroads we face. What hit me was the realization that every
decision is one that places us at specific crossroads. It takes us
either into balance or out of it a little further.

Crossroads are not, however, just matters concerning large
groups of people facing historic concerns. Primarily, they are, I
realized, the more specific decisions that affect my daily life, my
relationship with Christ, my family and friends.

Jake Spoon is a character in Larry McMurtry's book *Lonesome
Dove*. Jake makes an entire series of bad decisions at different
crossroads in his life. He chooses to flirt with another man's wife.
He chooses to get into a gunfight and kill a man. He chooses to
run. Later he chooses to join some outlaws who are unusually
evil. He chooses to be with them when they commit atrocities.
Finally, when all of them are captured, the inevitable result of
Jake's bad decisions comes to pass. Cal and Augustus, his former
Texas Ranger friends, execute Jake along with the others.

Before he is executed, however, Jake tries to plead his case:

"Pea, you know me," Jake said. "You know I ain't no
killer. Old Deets knows it, too. You boys wouldn't want to
hang a friend, I hope."

"I've done many a thing I didn't want to do, Jake," Pea Eye said.

Jake walked over to Augustus. "I ain't no criminal, Gus," he said. "Dan's the only one that done anything. He shot that old man over there, and he killed them families. He shot Wilbarger and his men. Me and the other boys have killed nobody."

"We'll hang him for the killing and the rest of you for the horse theft, then," Augustus said. "Out in these parts the punishment's the same, as you well know.

"Ride with an outlaw, die with him," he added. "I admit it's a harsh code. But you rode on the other side long enough to know how it works. I'm sorry you crossed the line, though."

"I never seen no line, Gus," he said. "I was just trying to get to Kansas without getting scalped."

There it is—the crossroads crisis that catches you and me. Jake didn't really participate, he claims, in the worst of the evils. He slid into the situation. He just made some wrong choices. He was just in the wrong company. He denied that he was responsible. But the reality was that each choice he made set the course for his ultimate destruction. He had become the victim of his own subtle choices.

I was brought up Catholic, and after each confession, I was taught to say a prayer that contains the line, "I further resolve with the help of Thy grace to sin no more and to avoid the near occasion of sin." I have always thought that was a powerful line. It puts the responsibility squarely on us. While I never have felt fully capable of living up to that prayer, of being able literally to "sin no more," it still hits home. You see, I know of several situations where my stumbles, my acts of sinning, have resulted from my failure to face up to the crossroads and avoid the "near occasion of sin."

The alcoholic knows that the first drink is one too many. My problem is dieting. If I try to diet, I had better not stock the house with cookies and ice cream. Each little crossroad reveals a decision to be made. Some of us "go along with the crowd" and find ourselves in places where we never would go alone. Choices about the company we keep and the places we go are crucial. We must weigh these apparently simple choices. *We must decide.* Where are the crossroad issues?

Choosing Christ is a crossroad moment. As the Bible verse at the beginning of this chapter implores, we must "enter through the narrow gate." Realistic words, aren't they? They tell of our crossroads.

There are so many choices that influence our lives: choosing friends, choosing a mate, choosing a church community, choosing how to use our time to serve the Lord. But these are just the larger decisions. Here is our catch: Each small, minidecision places you and me farther down a road that will have enormous consequences.

Crossroads—slippery, disguised, morally loaded, and vitally important. As I ponder this subject, Robert Frost's refrain keeps running through my mind:

> Two roads diverged in a wood, and I,—
> I took the road less traveled by,
> And that has made all the difference.

And I pray, "Lord, show me the right road to take in even the smallest crossroad moments of my life. Show me the path toward a new sense of balance."

# 4

# WHY GO TO CHURCH?
## DISCOVERING WHAT CHURCH
## IS ALL ABOUT

*Remember the sabbath day, and keep it holy.*

Exodus 20:8

Why do we go to church? Why do we even try? It is so
hard sometimes." These words of exasperation were flowing out
of my wife's mouth, but they were only echoing the cries in my
head. We rushed past cars on the freeway, trying to keep our
appointment with God. It had not been a good morning. And,
add this painful fact—it had not been a good night before.

Haydon, our four-year-old, had unaccountably turned into a
night owl. He had risen several times to renegotiate the terms of
his sleeping arrangements. His mother and father were too tired
to fight back. He climbed in and took over! As a result of this
exercise in musical beds, neither Kay nor I had obtained a good
night's sleep. After a hectic week, we both had needed sleep,
and we were still exhausted.

Over the years, our kids have succeeded in sleeping out of
their own rooms as much as in them. We have tried threats,
bribes, and physical punishment. On the positive side, we have
read bedtime stories until it was all we could do to stay awake
ourselves. Theory held that it would make them feel all warm
and fuzzy, so they would toddle off to sleep. We have tried it

all: lights on and lights off, star charts, even offers of bubble gum. We sounded like politicians offering promises of special treats and, like military generals, we have carried out our threats of punishment. Through all the frustrations and laughter, we have finally come to realize that our best bet is just time itself. With our third child, I pray that his required wandertime will set new records for brevity.

We have a friend whose children always slept through the night. I could not believe it. I wondered secretly whether she possessed some miracle drug or some outlandish treatment that could accomplish this goal.

One day I asked her, "Mary Ellen, why is it that your kids always sleep through the night?"

"Oh, I made up my mind a long time ago," she laughed, "that if my kids got up in the middle of the night, the last thing they would want to see was my face!" I am not sure what she looked like in those first few early morning confrontations, but it must have worked!

Why do we even try to go to church? I was really in a foul mood. Since I had not had enough sleep, I had tried to stay longer in bed. Thus I had arisen later than I should, too late for a leisurely reading of the Sunday paper over a cup of coffee. If I want to read the paper in peace—I mean real peace—I need to get up at the crack of dawn, before our little night owls start stirring. Once they awaken, they take over. Their cries for attention make reading the paper almost as impossible as climbing the Himalayas.

It was too late. I knew it. But I desperately needed my own routine. Even though it was later than usual, it was at least still dark. That much was hopeful.

I tried to drink my coffee and read about the President's call to sacrifice—pretty heavy stuff. Suddenly a wail split the air. Haydon needed the light on so he could use the bathroom. After that, he wailed some more because he could not have the bubble gum I had promised as a bribe *if* he slept in his bed all night. Had he, in fact, slept in that bed? Of course not. The fact that he had not slept in his bed had no bearing on the issue. According to his sense of injustice, the bed had nothing to do with it. I was simply depriving him of the promised gum.

That wasn't all. Our five-year-old daughter, Leigh, came into the picture. She asked not once, not twice, but repeatedly, When was I going to let her clean my teeth?—I say *my* teeth—with her new Cabbage Patch dentist kit. Great thing to hear first thing in the morning. I finally gave up, went downstairs, and let her take over as my dentist. Following this, I put my mind in neutral, gave up on the paper, and regrettably started getting dressed.

If we were going to get to church on time, we had to hop to it. We didn't have a minute to spare. In fact, I suddenly remembered that I was supposed to be chalice bearer at the service. Yipes! No time at all. I looked down at Leigh's feet then, only to discover that something was wrong. Unbelievably, she was wearing the ragged, worn-out soccer shoes of our oldest son, Eric. I frantically searched for her church shoes amidst the piles of toys, dolls, and clothes all over the floor of her room. I knew that I was doomed. I would be late, so late that someone else would be called on at the last minute to be the chalice bearer in my place.

Then I could just hear some old busybody, after reading my name in the church bulletin and seeing someone else up front, remark out loud, "You would think the Senior Warden of the church would not neglect to show up for this duty. What kind of example is he trying to set?"

I tore through her stuff. Good grief. To make matters worse, the problem was compounded—none of her clothes were in place. We were redoing her room and Kay had been painting her cabinets the day before.

Finally, shoes found, people hustled into the car, we were underway. Fifteen minutes behind schedule, the two little ones took turns reverting to their baby state, competing to see who could goo goo loudest. It was at that point that Kay exclaimed, "Why do we even try to go to church?"

I understood her frustration totally. In addition, I knew that Kay was not even going to be able to worship quietly with the other adults. She had volunteered for a new program in which parents of four- and five-year-olds were to spend one Sunday a month looking after them for two hours, so that the other parents would be able to worship, free of their squirming children. This was Kay's Sunday to work with the children. She would have to spend two hours doing what she does all week—corralling little children. No wonder she was questioning our choice of Sunday-morning activities, and probably her sanity as well.

I also wondered whether she was doing what I was doing at that moment. In my mind, I was miles away, thinking about last week's Sunday morning, when she and I had been alone together in a nice hotel in Dallas. It had been a weekend getaway. There we were, eating our continental breakfast and lingering over our paper and coffee. No rush. No lost shoes. We had all the time in the world before our 2:00 P.M. flight back to the reality of our lives. Beautiful. Besides, we had not gone to church that morning.

As we continued the drive to church, her question kept ringing in my ears. Why do we go to church? Why do we put ourselves through this each Sunday morning? Was it something left over from childhood, something still haunting us from those early years when a couple of well-intentioned teachers had frightened us about not going to church? Was it because of the "honor the Sabbath" admonition from the Bible? Was it because going to church was the "right thing to do"—the thing that solid citizens did? I wasn't as sure as I would have liked to be. I hoped that those were not the reasons I was rushing toward St. David's Episcopal Church, praying I would be only a little late.

A funny thing began to happen to me once I got to church. I settled into the pew and began to relax. As I sat there and looked around, I saw the beautiful windows and the arrangement of flowers at the altar. Strangely, I began to feel a sense of peace. As I felt led into the prayers, heard the reading of the Scriptures, reflected on the music by the choir, joined in singing the hymns, I realized that I was involved in something much greater than myself, some profound mystery.

I looked at the others around me and wondered why they had

come to church. There was the older woman who always beamed with such love and joy when she saw me and had assured me at critical times that we were in her prayers. And there was another, one who had become a highly respected pillar of the church. She had never married, but she had raised others' children, and now, standing alone and reading the prayers, she seemed so strong, and yet so in need of this place. Such a variety of people here—those in their Sunday best and those in blue jeans; the street person in the back who had wandered in; the young acolytes who only a year or two before had been in the sixth-grade Sunday school class. I saw those who were more conservative and those who were more liberal; some troubled by problems beyond control. Yet each person there this morning was searching for a relationship with God.

The sermon was based on the story of the Transfiguration. The minister talked about the time when, many years ago in seminary, he would not have believed that some day there would be women priests in The Episcopal Church. His point was that we need to see Christ as transfigured, empowered to transform the lives of others, if we are to see him revealed in them. In the prayers of the people, we gave thanks for the measure of healing that some of our congregation had received, and I was reminded of the fact that many others were still ill and in need of prayer.

When it was time for communion, we sang songs of praise, and my heart was lifted in the words:

> In Him there is no darkness at all.
> The night and the day are both alike.

I am not sure that I understood everything those words meant, but I was deeply touched by them.

During Sunday school, I saw old friends and met new ones. I was challenged by my teacher, who urged that we not limit our understanding of God and the role of pain in the world to that which we could comprehend. There was, I realized, a balance of faith and mystery.

As I approached Kay in front of the four-year-old room, I

wondered whether my positive attitude was about to be buffeted by new complaints about the burdens of the morning. How could Kay have gotten anything out of spending two hours with twelve four-year-olds? Would she resent the fact that I had been able to join others in worship?

Kay was not resentful. Instead, as soon as she saw me, she said, "You know, this is the first time I have been there to see our own two little ones in the children's service. They seemed so composed, so happy. And little Adam, he couldn't keep his eyes off me. Finally he came up and gave me a big hug and said, 'You brought us dinner last week. Thank you.' And I remembered that I had taken dinner to his family because his mother had recently gotten out of the hospital and was recovering at home." Kay's spirits were obviously lifted too.

Finally, after numerous hellos and good-byes, and kisses and hugs from friends, I whisked Kay and the kids into the car. Off we went to Wyatt's Cafeteria, where our Sunday dinner sometimes even resembled a family version of the food fight in the movie *Animal House*. Nevertheless, my attitude was different. Chaos and all, I think I understood the answer to the question, "Why do we go to church?" I felt that I had somehow rediscovered what church was all about.

As Christians, we truly are a family, a community, the Body of Christ, the people of God. We need to keep the Sabbath—to stop and rest and think each week about what we are doing, where we are going. And we need to do this in the community of believers where we can be fed on God's Word and be reminded of God's movement in our lives. There is no substitute for church. This is why Christians have been gathering in homes and churches from the beginning.

We are not a private religion. Yet there is a very private aspect to our faith. There is certainly a private part to everyone's faith, no one could overlook that. Many of us are determined to preserve it. However, what I had rediscovered was that there was a communal part to our interaction with others. As God's own power transfigured Christ, so his grace is still an awesome, transforming reality. And it often comes to us through others.

We need a private, personal relationship with God. But we also need others. We receive a sense of spiritual balance from one another. We need to be in a place where we can truly bear one another's burdens and share others' joys.

Our Sunday had begun with private frustrations, fatigue, and a definite feeling of resentment. If we had stayed home, gone to the mall, or parked the kids and played golf, I can tell you what I would have learned. I would have felt, at the end of the day, that something was still missing, still out of some subtle inward balance. I would have learned, once again, that we cannot live just off by ourselves.

On the other hand, I learned something positive from being in church. Part of this is that we have gone to church so long that I feel a personal openness, a spiritual sense of wonder there. I have learned that I have become a better person by being there. A sense of profound inner balance, a feeling of strength—however we describe it—I have discovered that even after a frazzled morning searching for a child's lost shoes, God himself comes to meet us. Is that not reason enough to set aside our frustrations and go there too?

# 5

# WHAT SEPARATES THE MEN FROM THE BOYS?

## UNPACKING THE MEDIA'S IMAGE OF A MAN

*When I was a child, I spoke like a child, I thought like a child, I reasoned like a child; when I became an adult, I put an end to childish ways.*

1 Corinthians 13:11

Everybody around me is a fitness nut. Even a heart patient that I know walks five miles at a time. Bodybuilders are more common than flies. Everyone wants to look strong. Not just healthy, I mean strong! So what really is strength? *Esquire* claims to know.

"*Esquire*—**It separates the men from the boys.**" So began the bold print on the flyer advertising this popular magazine. I hadn't read *Esquire* in years. Does anybody? So I wondered what was being promoted. Could *Esquire* possibly know what separates the men from the boys? At first the brochure spoke of the "search for excellence"—harmless enough. "It's about passion and pleasure. Excitement. Adventure. Fame. Fortune. Fun. It brings you life at its best. Your body at its best—in peak condition, superlative form. . . . And with the best writing published today." Unbelievable. Even considering advertising hyperbole, it was beyond credibility. I read on to see what else these publishers would say they perceived as the attributes of being a "man."

The flyer went on for two and a half pages of similar nonsense. What followed was a laundry list of notions supposed to characterize manly strength. Supposed to, I say, because they reminded me of a humanoid with all the real humanity scooped out. For example, "YOU KNOW . . . how to look at naked women—how to keep your hair forever. YOU KNOW IF . . . women would rather have more money, more power, or bigger breasts. YOU KNOW WHAT HAPPENS WHEN . . . you fake being a 'sensitive man.' " The advertisement described a "man" with a washboard abdomen, multiple sex partners, flashy cars, and luxury travel. It told me that if I read *Esquire*, I would know how "to be the right man at the right place at the right time." In short, I would have "the best." Big deal. Is that all? And would *Playboy* or *Penthouse* have taken it even further?

I have no doubt that this ridiculous advertisement is actually believed by many people. It seems incredibly ironic that such preoccupations, which in the past would have been considered obscene, if not immature, are now longingly sought as the ideal of what it means to be a male adult. "Adult Entertainment" has now become a marketing phrase. Look at the language we now use to describe movies and magazines that fit this category— language filled with some of the same things that formerly were considered generally unacceptable. But now they are called "adult," maybe because an adult has the legal freedom to choose such activities. But then again, it could mean that such trash scars children's minds more than the minds of adults. Whatever it means, calling it "adult" doesn't mean that it is by any genuine standard "mature." Does the truly mature person choose to tune in to such entertainment?

Books, magazines, songs, and movies that "push the envelope" on nudity, sexual conduct, violence, and language are hailed as daring, bold, innovative, or cutting-edge. But do they really indicate "maturity"? What they really do is sell us short on who we really are. No wonder a magazine like *Esquire* is compelled to produce such a brochure to compete for today's readers. As adults, as men, we have the freedom to make choices. What we are often lacking is the preparation, the quality we call "true maturity" to make best choices.

What separates the men from the boys? It's not just age. We all know that. It does involve age, but it also involves strength, determination, and a sense of balance. It involves making the mature, the right choices. It is accepting responsibility and living responsibly. It involves the capacity to sense what truly enhances and upbuilds the lives of others. It thus involves empathy as well as the ability to make moral distinctions and choices that are sometimes painful for us personally. It has a lot to do with faithfulness. It surely has nothing to do with full heads of hair, sports cars, flat stomachs, or voluptuous girl-friends.

When Paul spoke of giving up childish ways, he was giving us a tough order. But one thing he meant, I am sure, involved struggling with the self-centeredness of childhood. I have been watching this process of maturation in my own children. From the time of infancy, when the child believes that the world seems to revolve around his or her needs, each progresses into early childhood, where an awareness of the outer world begins to appear. Then gradually each learns to share, to exercise patience, to wait for one's own turn, to help others.

My wife and I are watching the unfolding of adolescence as our oldest child has gone off to school, returning to the United States from our temporary home in Kuwait. He is learning to take more and more responsibility for himself. This, of course, can be hard. The journey of maturation is not smooth and linear; it twists and turns and leads us down blind allies. It is some-times convoluted. But for him to become all that God ultimately means for him to be, he must make some critical choices. He must strive to gain the balance, to take the moral high ground, to be an increasingly responsible, caring, discerning person.

I worry about the cheap goals, the deceptive shortcuts, the contrary information that assail him; I have become an enemy of the trend today toward "self-actualization," and I hope that he will too. I fear the invasion of self-centeredness, of the focus on my needs, my career, my goals, my life, for I believe that it has produced a society in which the attitudes of the *Esquire* brochure go beyond mere advertising hyperbole to become what is thought of as reality. Thus, we are having to make tough choices, to choose what we accept and what we reject, to discover the real enemies of truth and goodness.

What separates the "men" from the "boys"? It involves the virtue of right choice. My father, the oldest of three boys, had dropped out of high school in the ninth grade to support his mom and brothers. His alcoholic father had left, and the burden of caring for the family had fallen on his small shoulders. He moved the family to another town and got a job at a drugstore as a clerk, a job he did well and carefully.

A doctor and his wife who frequented the store were childless and took a great liking to my dad. They had long dreamed of having a son who would go to medical school and join his father's practice. They approached my grandmother and offered to legally adopt Dad, send him to medical school, and give him every opportunity in life. My grandmother left the decision up to my father. Dad told me that the offer was really tempting. He had been an excellent student and loved school. He had been crushed when he had to drop out. The chance to become a doctor's son, to go to college and become a physician, was like an impossible dream. And yet, after much reflection, he did not accept. He stayed to take care of the family.

He never became a doctor; he never even got a college degree. But he also told me that he never regretted his decision. When faced with this life-changing choice at the ripe old age of fourteen, my father had the mature judgment to know what was right. My oldest child is now fourteen, and I think of him as a boy. But the choice my father made was a man's choice. Making the right choices, sacrificing for others, accepting responsibility—these qualities separate the "men" from the "boys."

I recently reread the old poem "If" by Rudyard Kipling and copied it to send to my son. Sure, it sounds out of date today. But I commend this work to anyone struggling with the question of what it means to be a man. Listen to this: Kipling talks about inner strength, about an in-depth capacity to "trust yourself when all men doubt you, but make allowance for their doubting," to recognize being lied about, but at the same time not "deal in lies," to know you are hated but not "give way to hating." These are the pillars of self-reliance, the strength for the soul, and the basic wisdom to go against the crowd and do what is right.

I want to share with you what I have discovered about inner strength. It has great promise for all of us. But we must reach out to claim it. We must adopt a new stance toward all that would deceive us. We must be their enemies. Then we must rebuild our lives with solid virtues. William J. Bennett's best-selling *The Book of Virtues* contains a wealth of wisdom about the characteristics of a mature man. It includes a list of building blocks for your soul's inner strength: self-discipline, compassion, responsibility, friendship, work, courage, perseverance, honesty, loyalty, faith. Put these spiritual vitamins into your inner life, and you'll know what really separates the men from the boys!

When I first read that list I felt overwhelmed. I looked *virtue* up in the dictionary and found the definitions I expected—quality of moral goodness, righteousness, responsibility. What surprised me was the seventh definition: "*Obsolete*. Manly courage, valor." *Something deep inside me suddenly came to life.* I wondered how this usage of the word had become obsolete! This connection offered the real secret: virtue and manliness were deeply linked! I read further. Buried in the definition was this truth, lying there like a diamond: the very word *virtue* derives from the "Latin *virtus*, manliness, strength, capacity, from *vir*, man."

*Esquire's* deceptive offer plays upon weakness. Its success depends upon convincing you that you are so weak inside yourself that you will jump at anything. True moral fitness, true manhood, and true inward strength go together. We can reclaim our personal strength. We can rebuild, no matter who may think we are weak. It is time we fought back, reclaimed and rebuilt the inward strength that our Creator meant for us to enjoy.

# 6

# I'M ONLY HUMAN...?

## ACCEPTING RESPONSIBILITY INSTEAD OF LOOKING FOR SCAPEGOATS

*Then God said, "Let us make humankind in our image, according to our likeness; and let them have dominion over the fish of the sea, and over the birds of the air, and over the cattle, and over all the wild animals of the earth, and over every creeping thing that creeps upon the earth."*

*So God created humankind in his image, in the image of God he created them; male and female he created them.*

Genesis 1:26-27

I'm only human." A bald-faced excuse—and thus a lie. How many times have we heard those words? Have we said them ourselves at some convenient time, when we were looking for an easy excuse? "No one is perfect." "Everybody makes mistakes." "We are all sinners." We have quite a litany of excuses when we fail. Most of the time, we do not even question the truth of these statements. We attribute our failures, our weaknesses to the fact that "we are only human." When we give up our sense of shame, we also give up the integrity of being human.

One of the worst abuses of this cliche can be found in the words of a song of the same name that was popular a few years ago. The man in the song has cheated on his wife. He is trying to explain what happened, to ask for forgiveness. He tells her, "I'm only human, born to make mistakes." His failure, his infidelity, is brushed off by this attempt to escape responsibility, this universal excuse that as humans, we should expect and accept failure as the norm. But that is not the end.

What makes this song even more troubling is the wife's response. It seems she also has had an affair. She tells him that while he was being human, she "was being human too." Sweet revenge; tit for tat; what is good for the goose is good for the gander. But this isn't the worst part. The real sinkhole here is that the excuse cuts the goodness right out of the heart—the goodness God put there—and throws it away.

I do not dispute the premise that all of us are sinners and make mistakes. That is self-evident. Once we look at ourselves from the perspective of the Christian faith, we see ourselves even more clearly. It is this very reality that creates in us the need for a Savior—for repentance, for forgiveness, for redemption. There is true hope in knowing that.

There is, of course, no hope for God's own work if we whine that we are sinners because "we are *only* human." This entirely cynical phrase diminishes the wonder, the majesty of being human, being created in the image of God, unique among all God's creatures. It dooms us to a flawed and base existence where a cycle of failure is inevitable, part of our human nature. Not to mention the fact that it represents an unbalanced view of the Christian faith.

The word *just* is about as dangerous to our minds as a triple dose of crack cocaine. I am reminded of a time when the use of this slippery little word got me into a lot of trouble with my wife. She was in the middle of a long and exhausting labor before the birth of our first child. Like a good father to be, I had gone to the child-birthing classes, and I took my job as "coach" very seriously. The time for the birth had finally come. As I dutifully timed each contraction, I kept trying to reassure my wife that everything would be okay.

"*Just* a few more seconds until this contraction is over," I would cheerfully intone. "*Just* a little while longer."

Finally, my exasperated wife yelled out, "If you say *JUST* one more time, I am going to kill you. *Just* implies that it is no big deal. Believe me, *THIS IS A BIG DEAL!*" Unfortunately for me, in the midst of my confusion, I made the mistake of responding that I was *just* trying to be helpful. I'm sure it was only the strength of the next contraction that prevented her from carrying out her threat and killing me then and there. She was right. *Just* implies that something is no big deal. It was just an accident, we say. It was just a physical act. It didn't mean anything.

Here is where *just's* synonym, *only*, slips in to trip us up too. As my wife was frustrated at my habitual insertion of the word *just* to describe the very serious events in that delivery room, I have become increasingly hostile to the knee-jerk use of the adjective *only* to describe what it means to be human. To put it bluntly, I have become an enemy to its use, in order to preserve what is noble about us! Surely we are human and not God; but we are made in God's image. What this means is great news for us. It means that God intends us to become good, to be holy, to live joyfully in God's likeness. Therefore we have no right to focus on our imperfections.

A Muslim friend told me that in their religion, they have a saying to the effect that angels were created with a mind but no desires; animals were created with desires but no mind. Therefore, it is only humans who have both mind and desire. When humans are ruled by their minds, they can do good that surpasses the works of angels. When humans are ruled by their desires, their evil exceeds anything in the animal world. I think there are much wisdom and truth in this saying.

It is time that we, as men, as Christians, put our minds to work. For our own benefit, we need to abolish the expression "I'm *only* human" from our speech. Let's face it, we've excused ourselves enough. We do not need more excuses for our failings. We have been down that street, and we know it is a dead end. What we need is more appreciation of what it means to be created in the image of God, redeemed by Christ, and inspired by the Holy Spirit. In this context, being human means that we have the will to choose our actions, our destiny. We are redeemed by Christ, and this means that now we need to choose how we live our lives. We need to take full responsibility for our choices, our actions.

The power of Christ leads us toward a restored and directed choice, but we must remember that we also have the freedom to fail. That freedom brings with it the freedom to experience the tremendous joy of success, of overcoming hardships and trying times. The freedom to sin gives the opportunity to *not* sin; to overcome temptation; to love and serve the Lord. Here, in dealing with this responsible choice, we discover what it really means to be a man. We also discover something more about the true balance in the Christian life.

We humans, made in God's image, have been given a unique privilege—the chance to become the living hands of Christ to do his work here on earth; love our neighbor; feed his lambs; share the Good News. We have the highest honor of submitting to and carrying out God's will. What an undeserved honor it is to be human! What a precious gift we have been given! Doubly blessed: created in God's image, redeemed by Christ. What a cause for celebration! What an opportunity! And this means that we do not need to remain as we have been. He separates our sin, as the psalmist says, as far as the East is from the West. Now we can choose that which is right and good. We must choose, in fact, if we are to be truly human. Here is a unique thing: In choosing for Christ, we regain what it is to be more than "only human." Thanks be to God!

# 7

# ON OUR OWN SPECIAL COURSE THROUGH TIME

## AGING, AND HOW TO AVOID BEING UNBALANCED BY OTHERS

*He has made everything suitable for its time.*

Ecclesiastes 3:11a

I received a call about ten years ago from my sister. At that time she had reached the ripe old age of forty-one, and her first-born son had just been involved in his first car accident.

"I don't believe it," she cried. "I'm not old enough to have a teenager who just wrecked our car!" Thankfully, her son was not seriously hurt, and she could joke about the passing of the years.

At the time, our oldest was only four, and I had not yet begun to worry about such things. They seemed a long way off. Car wrecks were not even on the radar screen of concerns. I was still at the point of watching over him on the playground, trying to let go enough so that he could climb the big slide by himself.

Now this son of mine will be fifteen in about two weeks. He talks continually about the car he wants when he turns sixteen. He knows exactly what he wants. Sometimes I wonder if he can even tear his eyes away from the car magazines long enough to eat. He begs for practice drives on the dirt roads near our home in Texas. Guess what! I have caught up with my sister. Her son, my oldest nephew, is now a man in his late twenties, with three kids of his own. Now my son is the one ready to drive. And I am the one who is forty-two years of age.

"For everything there is a season, and a time for every matter under heaven" (Eccles. 3:1). This has to be one of the most famous passages in the Bible. It is also the basis of a classic folk song still played on the radio from time to time. Whenever I hear it, time seems to reverse for a moment. Have you ever felt that? For just a moment, a fleeting instant, I can feel again what it was like to hear that when I was younger. When I am honest, I realize that I often rebel against the passing of time. Psychologists may call it regression. I just know that there have been times when I wanted to go back, to somehow relive or capture those experiences that still lurk in my memories, or even have a chance to enjoy the essence of experiences I did not have in my youth.

Much like George Burns' musical musings about wishing to be eighteen again, many of us fight this notion of aging, if only in our dreams. I admit that there are times when I rebel at the notion of getting older and I would give almost anything to rescript my life, to reenter those earlier years, to do it right this time.

I have done something daring. I have put all these longings down on paper. And more, much more—private stuff. Every day, when time allows, I write it all out in my own journal. Why go to all this trouble? So I can read and reread my thoughts and experiences. It's scary at times, but those journals hold a kind of key to my life. Rereading them from time to time may seem to be weird, but it gives me a reality check. It opens up to me in an odd sort of way the rhythms and patterns of my life. Amazing parallels occur. If something is really bothering me, I go back into an earlier journal to see what was happening about the same time of year, five years before. Surprising results come from this. Reading about crises resolved or hardships overcome enables me to see today's events in a better, more balanced framework, a different perspective. Often, I am surprised that I had forgotten all about a similar crisis faced in the earlier journal.

There was one time in particular, one moment recorded in the journal, that really hit me. It showed how rebellious I have been at submitting to the seasons of my life. It also showed something about the importance of physical appearance in our self-esteem—especially when we are young—how easy it is to adopt the old stereotype of "real men" as jocks. I wrote this entry when I was in my early thirties and thought I was "getting old." I can smile now and wish I were thirty-three again. I titled it "What Would Have Happened to Rudolph If It Had Not Been Foggy That Christmas Eve?" It began like this:

*Saturday, December 5, 1987, 2:40 P.M.*

I am sitting in my room at the Four Seasons Hotel. We are using the weekend getaway I bought at the Arthritis Foundation Ball Charity Auction. My wife is out running errands.

This afternoon I went to the hotel health club to exercise. There was only one other man working out. He was younger, shorter, more muscular, more "jock" looking. The way I guess I wish I looked.

Physical appearance is important to us. I am not in high school playing football. I am not competing for popularity. I am in better shape than most people my age. Yet appearance is important.

We never get through the phase of wanting to feel accepted. Guys who were jocks did not try to have those things. They just came naturally. Oh, some worked out more with weights, but the basic build was there, and it came at the time when it was important for them and their friends. This was especially true in my small school where everyone seemed to play football. Those who played on a team belonged. The rest of us didn't.

Here is the odd thing: I still envy these people years later. Those student athletes seemed to have a permanent status that goes on, even if they end up dead broke. Even if they get pot bellies and bald heads. They are free to lose their bodies, have disastrous careers, marry incredibly wrong people, and yet never lose the self-image that comes from having accomplishments that I never had. Can you explain it? Maybe part of it comes simply from that male bonding thing, the power of being on the team together. Sure, everyone gripes. Even the former athletes complain—old injuries crying out still, physiques caving in, fat grams galore. But they know that they once looked great. And in their minds, ironically, they belong again.

Here I am, thirty-three, in good shape. I work out fanatically; I watch what I eat—low caloric stuff that tastes like mud. I even ran in a marathon this year. I am truly more muscular than when I was nineteen, and I look better than I ever have. Truly. And yet I still feel out of sync. I have the sensation of having arrived at a party at the same time everyone else is going home. Here is the really ironic part of this thing. I believe that I am finally trying to be the jock I never was, in order to belong to a group I never belonged to. Still trying! Even when that group is gone!

So what I am really doing is actually separating myself from my own age-appropriate group all over again. I am the odd one once more, having by some weird quirk of fate missed the boat a second time. I can't win. I wasn't an athlete when it counted. I am one when it doesn't. Yet to give up, to get out of shape, to be fifty pounds overweight, still will not let me in the club, at least not all the way. Why not? It is apparently this—I do not have and will never have the shared memories—the touchdown run that won the game, the triple at the district playoffs. I know it's crazy, but memories persist that way.

Most people do not have these memories. Few people really do, but somehow I am still haunted by the loss. So I see a younger man who is athletic, confident in his appearance, seemingly well put together, and I get this pain, this sinking feeling in my stomach that working out harder will not change my situation. It will not make me twenty and confident. It will not really make me feel more self-assured about my looks. It will not give me the camaraderie of the good old boys. The twenty-year-olds will still see me as approaching middle age, in good shape "for my age." And all of this fitness-crazy working out will only separate me from my own generation. A day late and a dollar short. Friends my age will see me as a little odd to be so obsessed with physical appearance, so long after most of my generation has moved on emotionally, regrettably but realistically accepting their changing bodies.

What is the solution? Try to avoid the changes of time, or give up and become old? How do I derive pleasure from my appearance, but relief from the pressure to attain a perfect body? Well, attaining goals can be good. I did get a lot of satisfaction out of running twenty-six miles to finish the marathon. I knew I had accomplished something special. I felt great afterwards, physically alive and proud to be able to achieve something that most others could not.

But it was a hollow victory. It was just the way it felt years ago; it was just the same as the feelings of a little kid who, when he was excluded from playing with the other kids, climbed the unclimbable tree—did something they could not do. "I'll show them!" he vowed. And when he succeeded, he might have been proud, but pride does not create friendships or acceptance. It hurt then; it hurts now.

So here is where Rudolf the deer with the odd nose comes into the picture. Not everyone who is different is as lucky as Rudolf, who received acceptance because of a wonderful Santa, who can appreciate a shiny red nose on a foggy night. In fact, I often wonder what would have happened to Rudolf if it had not been a foggy night?

And so ended my early-thirties journal entry. It's dangerous to put down your thoughts. I can look back on it now with a mixture of pain and amusement. After all, the truth is that we don't really have a choice. The reality of the passage of time forces us to deal with the fact that we are getting older. And we have a lot to gain, a new balance about our lives, when we come to terms with this creatively. Younger men, like the one I saw in the hotel gym and wrote up in my journal musings, now really do consider me much closer to the age of their father than their older brother. I have less energy and less hair than I used to have. I am even well aware of how much "younger" I was when I wrote those words in my journal. When I talk with my seventy-year-old father, I realize, in an entirely different way, that time passes. Dad tells me that he believes his favorite decade was his fifties!

Is there a lesson for me, and perhaps for others, in the complaints of my youthful journal entry? I think it might help. When I read it today, I am struck by how self-absorbed I was, and how self-absorbed I remain. At the same time, and even more painfully, I see reflected in that entry the remarkable degree to which my self-image is colored by my perceptions of others and by the assumptions I make about their views of me. Acceptance is like a drug. I am a slave to others' acceptance, and I seem to equate their approval with conformity to some perceived stereotype. Much like anyone who never wants to seem different, who wants to live in the right neighborhood, drive the right car, wear the right clothes, the one driven to conform loses more than he gains. You lose your balance, for conformity can be an abdication of your freedom. It can leave you unbalanced, always blown off course by the whims of others—not a place we want to be.

I have much to learn if I am to accept myself as I am, as a child of God, to find an assurance somewhere within that cannot be shaken, that endures through the changes of time. I see this when I reread my journal entry. The funny thing is that my own teenage son seems to be working on this too. He called this morning from school.

"Guess what, Dad? I shaved my head!" he blurted out.

"Shaved your head?" I repeated.

"Yeah! You see, a couple of the guys in the dorm kept talking about it, but they kept chickening out, and well, I just got tired of all the jabbering, so I went into the bathroom, got the razor and—no hair!"

"No hair at all?" I replied. "What did everyone say?"

Then I realized what I had done. I had responded in knee-jerk concern that my son would be rejected by doing this, that he would then feel separated for life.

"Some think it's cool, some weird, but I like it, so who cares?" he responded. "And besides, now my roommate has shaved his head. Who knows, maybe I'll start a trend."

Maybe. He may never start anything remotely resembling a trend. But he doesn't know that yet. One day we both may truly learn that starting or following trends won't help us much. One thing only remains; to discover that there is a God who cares very much for exactly what is in the very deepest parts of our souls. God wraps around us when the wind blows and keeps us right on balance, on our own special course. We belong to God, and that is enough!

# 8

# HOW DEEP IS YOUR RUDDER?

## KEEPING YOUR BALANCE AGAINST THE PREVAILING WINDS

*He woke up and rebuked the wind, and said to the sea, "Peace! Be still!" Then the wind ceased, and there was a dead calm. He said to them, "Why are you afraid? Have you still no faith?"*

Mark 4:39-40

We met at a health club. He was a University of Texas senior, but to my surprise, he was training for the Boston Marathon. Against great odds, he also had landed a job with a Wall Street investment banking firm and was headed for New York upon graduation.

We decided to run together that day, and as we ran we talked. I was impressed with his maturity, his sense of self. I asked why he seemed so sure of himself, so comfortable with both the present and the future. He remarked that he had attended boarding high school and attributed some of his independence to that experience. He also explained that he was the youngest of five, and his parents had provided a very stable and nurturing environment for their family.

As we continued to talk, I discovered that, like me, he kept a journal in which he chronicled the days of his life; that he was a Christian, and his faith was important to him. As I looked at him, I saw myself as a college student, so eager to gain admission to a law school and become a successful lawyer some day. I also saw an image of my older son, as I hoped he would be in a few years: confident, self-assured, ready to take on the world. I hoped that I was doing my part to prepare my son for that time in his life.

My new friend continued to describe his siblings, all of whom had established themselves in the world in some responsible fashion. I thought of my three children, and how I hoped that they also would grow to be responsible adults, able to take care of themselves as well. Finally, at the end of the run, this student noted that, in many ways, his mother was his role model. He used the example of a sailboat to describe her.

"She has a deep rudder," he said. "She knows who she is and does not let the storms around her blow her off course. If you are sailing in really rough seas, you have to have a deep rudder to steer; if you don't, as the waves come and the boat is lifted up and down, the rudder won't hold, and you can't steer. I keep working on deepening my rudder. I want to be like her. That is why I really did not get uptight about this job business. I knew the odds were overwhelmingly against me landing this job in New York, but I knew I would be all right either way; and I think that confidence may have come across in the interviews."

I thought to myself that I was sure it had.

As the days passed, I thought about the image of the boat and the importance of having a deep rudder to guide you in life. I remembered an experience from an Outward Bound adventure course I had taken a few years before. We were sailing off the coast of Maine. We were all novice sailors, and our two instructors had spent a couple of days teaching us the fundamentals of sailing the antiquated wooden boat that had become our home.

The day had arrived for us to sail by ourselves, without instruction from our teachers. We were told to raise the sails and set a course that would take us around an island. As we struggled to keep on course, the winds from the ocean side of the island hit us broadside time after time and almost blew us over. The instructors sat silently at the back of the boat, saying nothing as they watched us scramble to bark out conflicting orders and try to handle the wind-driven sails. Finally we succeeded in bringing the boat around, completing the course, and anchoring it in a harbor out of the wind. We were exhausted, but proud. The ocean wind had come at us, but we had handled it. We were sure that we had sailed through what must have been a gale-force storm. But we had proved that we could do it. We knew what we were doing.

As we sat around congratulating ourselves and reliving harrowing moments, one of the instructors remarked that the trip would have been infinitely easier if we had dropped our keel in the water before we set sail. The keel runs from the front to the back of the boat and forms the backbone of the ship. On the small boat we were sailing, you had to raise the keel when you were in shallow water, and once you set sail, lower it. It was only then that we realized that we had misconstrued the whole situation.

The reason it had seemed so hard was not due to the wind. In fact, it hadn't been that bad. The reason was that without the keel, the boat had no depth and was easily tossed about by the waves and the wind. Our instructors had been there. They could have reminded us, but that is not what they chose to do. They wanted us to take responsibility for the trip. One day, we would in fact sail without them. They had drilled us on the proper techniques, and they wanted us to use them. They had given us the knowledge, but we did not use it.

Keels and rudders. A ship needs both—the keel for strength and stability, the rudder to set the course. People are like ships. We need to use both our keels and our rudders. We have to know who we are and where we are going, or we will crash. All of us have seen the consequences, the shipwrecked and shattered lives.

As I recalled that sailing incident, I thought of how I sometimes react to the storms of life as if I do not have my keel in the water or a deep rudder to steer through the crashing waves. I forget how to get where I am going, or I lose the ability to steer across the currents of life. Instead, I tend to put my head down and stubbornly struggle against the wind, without really knowing where the struggle is taking me. I get caught up in the crisis of the moment, and it is easy to lose sight of the larger goals in my life. Without a keel, something deep down in the water, centering me, I can become fearful that I will be blown over, like the apostles who had to awaken a sleeping Jesus because they feared the storm. And unless I have a deep, strong rudder in the water, I know I can't really set a true course to my long-term destination.

How do we make sure our keels are always set deep in the water to give us balance? And how do we put down deep rudders, as my young runner friend advised? I think that, much like the unused keel of my sailing adventure, we have the tools to center us, but they have not been fully used. We haven't really dropped our keel in the water, and we don't fully understand how to use our rudder in the stream of our lives. The Bible, like a keel, can form the backbone of our ship. Likewise, the Bible can be used as a kind of rudder that is always there, at our ready disposal. The Bible contains all the wisdom needed to form a foundation to govern our lives and guide us against the currents that pull at us. It contains the principles to help us make the right choices when the storms of life threaten to overtake us.

Christ tells us that loving God and loving our neighbors as ourselves sums up all of the Law. The Ten Commandments prescribe a way of life that is so plain, so basic, that the answers to many of life's issues can be found in these instructions: love God and God only; honor parents; tell the truth; respect the things of others; be satisfied with what is ours and do not envy the blessings of others; remember to worship our God and to rest and keep holy the Sabbath; and respect the sanctity of our relationships with our spouses. If we are really struggling in some of these areas of our lives, maybe we need to check to see whether we have dropped our keel and are using the rudder that we already have, the knowledge that has been set out for us in Scripture. We need to use these essential tools.

When we put the Scripture to use, two basic things begin to happen. One is simply that we discover in both the Old and the New Testament an outline of a way of life, a basic philosophy of the Great Commandments of love of God and neighbor that can guide our decisions in the day-to-day affairs of our lives. The second is that we become better acquainted with God as revealed in Jesus. He isn't asleep. He is very much involved in our lives. His Spirit guides us through His Word.

I think we can go a step further to be sure we have our keels firmly set in the water and deep rudders to steer us. Through journal writing, which really isn't that hard, we gain much clarity about where we are in our lives. Keep it going daily, if possible. And there is another simple tool—a mission statement. Through a prayerful articulation of a personal mission statement, we can set forth for ourselves: who we are as persons; how we relate to our wives, children, parents, friends, coworkers; and how we are trying to live our lives in balancing the responsibilities we all face. It may sound a little strange, but it really does help. Write it out. A mission statement in itself, prepared in a time of calm, provides a kind of rudder. Remember it. Perhaps keep a copy with your Bible. Have it at your work. You can turn back to this tool when the crises come. The mission statement prepared in the spirit of biblical truths can help us make right decisions.

The more we put the Scripture to use in such ways as a genuine keel and rudder, the more we will sense that we are not on our own. Jesus Christ will help us. He will be there, and if we use our biblical wisdom regularly, He will help us to keep our balance and stay on course. We all need a strong keel in the water and the deepest rudder we can find. We are facing currents that we never knew would be there to threaten us. We can easily get blown off course and struggle much harder than we ever dreamed, when we ignore the watchful Instructor sitting with us in the boat, wondering why we have forgotten to put down the keel or use the rudder He gave us in the lessons He taught, but letting us struggle on, so that we will learn.

Do you have your keel in the water to keep you balanced against the prevailing winds? Do you have a deep rudder to steer with and keep you on course? Do you use these tools to provide a truthful sense of self and purpose for your life? These are important questions that we need to ask ourselves every day. I know I do.

# 9

# HAVE YOU PUT GOD IN A BOX?

## MAKING ROOM FOR GOD IN YOUR WORK

*But the leader of the synagogue, indignant because Jesus had cured on the sabbath, kept saying to the crowd, "There are six days on which work ought to be done; come on those days and be cured, and not on the sabbath day."*

Luke 13:14

As I write this book, I am living and working in Kuwait, a Muslim country where the concept of separation of church and state is an anathema. The constitution and laws are supposed to be based upon the religious laws. I have gained a tremendous respect for the Muslim religion. There are many things about these people's depth of faith and commitment to God that I admire. But I sense that some of them have also reformulated a box for God's will, a tight box of social customs and rules. When they feel that this box is threatened, especially by the pluralism and social norms and values of the West, they seek to impose their concept of God's will by attempting to legislate a social agenda that is hard for someone from the West to understand. As I read debates in the paper about whether religious law requires women to be veiled or the sexes to be segregated from kindergarten through college, I begin to understand the climate of Jesus' time, what he was up against. Once God is in a box, once one thinks that all the rules are set out only to be discovered, the focus of the debate can go from the sublime to the ridiculous.

I read a couple of days ago that a religious teacher in a neighboring country issued an edict against women wearing high heels. He argued that they were forbidden because they were intended to make the women more attractive to men. This edict was issued in a place where women were already prohibited from working in most professions, from driving or even traveling about if they were not veiled. The whole debate ranked right up there with the uproar caused in Kuwait when a religious leader issued an edict against Barbie dolls. In this case, the problem was that they were too anatomically correct, and this might lead to bad thoughts. Perhaps little girls could be corrupted by the things they might think as they played. Heaven forbid, they might want to dress in a Western fashion that would imitate Barbie!

In this context, putting God in a box means assuming we really can understand far beyond the general revelation of God's love in Scripture, a far more detailed application of God's will in all situations. The Pharisees of Jesus' time placed their energies, their focus, on precisely defining and protecting the law. Jesus said that they had missed the boat. He called them hypocrites who "tithe mint, dill, and cummin, and have neglected the weightier matters of the law: justice and mercy and faith. . . . You blind guides! You strain out a gnat but swallow a camel!" (Matt. 23:23b, 24).

But what about us in the West? Have we put God in a box? Of course. Only it is a different kind of box. It is in fact even more restrictive. Where Jesus' contemporaries sometimes thought that they knew exactly what God wanted of them, they at least thought he wanted something. We seem to think that what God really wants is to be left alone—left out, if not put out of our lives. And you and I are happy to oblige him. Our box for God is Sunday religion. It is a subtle thing. The more God's box is restricted to Sunday-type affairs, the more we leave him out of other areas of our lives. Sometimes we are determined to purge public life of any civic recognition of God. We see litigation to prevent Christmas displays that have been erected for years. While there are constitutional issues, it has gone too far. Isn't it profoundly symbolic that Christian groups need to file lawsuits to win the right to meet on public-school campuses, where other organizations have been meeting without question and regardless of their agendas?

Think about this: We have even expelled God from any positive role in our daily language. Living in the Muslim world, I have learned some of the phrases in the Arabic language. What I discovered is that there is still a kind of gentle piety in Arabic. The daily expressions of greeting and departing sound almost like the liturgies in our church. Loosely translated, they mean "Peace be with you," "God's peace be with you too," and "Go with God." When someone asks how you are doing, the minimum reply is, "Thanks be to God." Surely, this could easily be taken for granted. People could forget the religious meaning. But I think it symbolizes something important: God is everywhere.

In our language, it seems that the only time we hear God's name anymore is when it is taken in vain. We have unconsciously banished God from everyday language. In fact, I was pleasantly surprised to hear an American standing near me at the airport baggage claim carousel the other day say to his friend who had inquired about his bags, "God willing, they will be here soon." I could hardly believe my ears. It was such an exception. Later on, someone came up to the man and handed him a book he had left on the plane. "Thanks be to God" was his reply. Then I glanced at the book. It was the Holy Bible, and it was well worn.

I sense this feeling deep inside: Our society is increasingly trying to put God in a box, a Sunday-religion box, where he won't interfere with our daily lives. And when we are honest about this, many of us feel that something serious has gone wrong. Something is missing from our lives as men. Many men, I think, unconsciously subscribe to the Pharisees' understanding that there is one set of rules for the working, social world, and another set for Sunday. We just do not make the connection between the Sunday God of religion and family, and the Monday work world. So I have made a radical decision. I want to reestablish a balance in these worlds, to bring them together. I want to straighten this out, and somehow rediscover the place for God in my professional life.

As I was driving to work one morning, I was preoccupied with the dilemma of how to increase my productivity at work. Like many other men, I had bought and listened to time-management and motivational tapes. I had made daily lists of things to do. I had tried reprioritizing things. And yet, I sometimes still found it hard to stay on track, to get everything done, to keep myself on schedule. I always felt that I should be doing more.

Shortly before I arrived at the office, a thought occurred to me. Why had I never prayed about this problem? I pray often and about many personal things. I pray for healing, for family concerns, for friends in need, and even for world problems. I also pray prayers of praise and thanksgiving; but as I reflected upon my prayer life, I could not remember ever praying about my job. I asked myself, why? I believe it was because I did not see God's place in the "secular" part of my life. Sunday religion hadn't seemed to be as appropriate in the realm of tough decisions. I realized that ever since I had "gotten this job for myself," I had shut God out of this part of my life. I had compartmentalized my life into those areas where I thought I needed God's help, and those areas that were my own. Sound familiar?

How could I have been so blind for so long? Who knows? Maybe we leave God in our society's special Sunday box so long that we think he belongs there. Then we stop thinking about it at all. Too busy, too focused. Automatic pilot turns on, and we continue down the same path, the same familiar way of looking at things. Do we get too caught up in pride? My wife says that I can't even ask someone for directions. How much more might pride keep me from turning to God? After all, wasn't I a reasonably successful lawyer? Hadn't I jumped through all the hoops, made the contacts, gotten the job? Surely I should be able to solve work-related problems by myself.

I believe the Holy Spirit used that contemplative moment to "knock me off my horse," to tell me that no part of my life is mine alone. I realized that I needed God in all of my life, every facet. The first way I could acknowledge this need was to pray immediately that God would help me in my work, that he would help me do the best job possible. I felt that I wanted to offer my work to him, to give him the glory. I resolved to highlight my work in my prayer life every day. I am certain that Jesus the carpenter can understand all the challenges and frustrations of my work. I need to lean on his shoulder and ask for his strong arms to support me as much in my work as in my personal life.

To help me in this task, I wrote out a prayer, a Businessman's Prayer, and I have tried to pray it daily ever since. You are welcome to it. Feel free to change it or add anything to it that might help you.

## A BUSINESSMAN'S PRAYER

God, be with me this day in all of my life. Do not let me shut you out of any part. I need you in my work as well as in my personal life. I need to turn to you in praise as well as in sorrow, in joy as well as in sadness.

I need you in my marriage and all of my relationships. I need you in my inner struggles, too. In the depths of my soul, I cry out for help, for forgiveness, and for renewal.

Help me to accept both life's blessings and life's struggles, neither boasting nor complaining. Free me from the slavery of seeking the approval of others. Let me live simply and completely, with a forgiving heart and an open mind.

Lord, help me learn to listen—to you, to my wife, to my children, to my friends, to my colleagues. Grant me patience, compassion, and perseverance. Teach me to accept and love myself, so that I can love others.

My job requires much effort, and I need your guidance. Keep me productive and free from doubt and worry. Help me to do a good day's work, and then leave it behind. Help me find time for all that must be done, a discerning mind and heart to accomplish what can be done, and to accept what cannot be accomplished in this twenty-four-hour day.

Most of all, give me the joy for life that comes only from the movement of the Holy Spirit in my life. Lift me up and sustain me with your love, and at the end of this day, grant me peace and a carefree mind, secure in the knowledge of your love. Amen.

# 10

# DOES GOD CARE ABOUT MY WORK?

## ASKING TOUGH QUESTIONS WHEN THE SACRIFICE DOESN'T SEEM WORTH IT

*There [Paul] found a Jew named Aquila, a native of Pontius,*
*who had recently come from Italy with his wife, Priscilla,*
*because Claudius had ordered all Jews to leave Rome. Paul*
*went to see them, and, because he was of the same trade, he*
*stayed with them, and they worked together—by trade they*
*were tentmakers. Every sabbath he would argue in the syna-*
*gogue and would try to convince Jews and Greeks.*

Acts 18:2-4

When my dad was in his late thirties, he lost his business, went bankrupt, and had to move his family to Tyler, Texas. Two of my uncles who sold oil-field equipment got my dad a job as a "roughneck," explaining that in a few years after he had learned the trade, they would get him a job as a salesman. So there he was, overweight, out of shape, a heavy smoker, sweating in the oil fields with men twenty years younger. It was extremely tough work. Nevertheless, he persevered until one day he was almost killed by a hammer that dropped from a rig. At that point, having proved himself, he decided that he did not really belong in the oil fields.

Even so, he remains very proud of the fact that before he left, his boss had told him, "Cameron, I just want you to know that you have made an oil-rig hand." He had proved that he could do it. It had taken plain work and much personal sacrifice. There isn't a lot of room for self-actualization in the oil fields.

After that, Dad did everything possible in order to pay the bills. Odd jobs, including sacking groceries at a nearby store, helped provide for his family until he landed a job as a salesman for a wholesale company that sold meat to restaurants and other establishments. For many years he was their top salesman, and today, at age seventy, he is still working for them. As is often the case, here is a man who has worked harder than his own son, and probably will have worked longer when he retires. I admire his work ethic, the way he accepts the sacrifice of work, and also the way he gains a feeling of accomplishment from it.

Does God care about our work? The Apostle Paul was probably the greatest Christian evangelist of all time. The spread of Christianity, from its beginning as a small community of Jewish believers to the world religion it has become, can be traced in large measure to the missionary zeal of that incredibly gifted man. And yet Paul was a tentmaker. He was also a tradesman. He always wanted to pay his own way, not to be a burden. In his first letter to the Corinthians, he went to great lengths to explain that even though as a teacher, he was entitled to his wages, he refused to earn his living this way because he wanted to present the gospel free of charge. Paul had a clear sense of the value of honest work and the respect that people gave it.

I am sure that Paul also affirmed that this was critical to his calling as a Christian. Thus he probably would have said that your work matters to God. And if this is the case, if our work, whatever it might be, really makes a difference to God, wouldn't that be the most incredible thing? It would lead to all kinds of questions, especially for Christians. What is the role of sacrifice in our work and our faith? Should our work normally include certain sacrifices for the well-being of others? How far should one go? Does God intentionally place us in circumstances where personal sacrifices are necessary? These are all difficult questions as I struggle with the meaning of work in my life and its relationship to God.

I sometimes wonder if we, as relatively affluent people, are beginning to forget the meaning of sacrifice and its impact on our growth.

Ruth Stafford Peale once wrote that after her freshman year, she had to drop out of college and take a job to help support her older brother's college education. It seems that the family had gotten together and determined that they could not afford to send both children to school that year. The decision had been made that Ruth would have to work. The plan was that when her brother graduated, he would help pay for her education. She understood it, took it in good spirit, and accepted her duty. Of course, she had not wanted to postpone her education, to spend a year in a job she did not particularly like. But sacrifice for the family, for her brother, was expected. It was the thing to do. She went on to explain that God had used this delay in her education to change her life profoundly. If she had not graduated a year later than planned, she never would have met Norman Vincent Peale, her husband of more than forty years. Hard work, sacrifice, and strong family ties—these three principles seemed to guide her life, as they had my father's. However, I wonder if they are less prevalent in today's more affluent and self-absorbed society.

As I reflected upon Ruth Peale's story, I thought again about my father and his life. He married when he was seventeen. By the time he was eighteen, he had become a parent himself and was drawn into the war. At nineteen, he was injured at Guadalcanal and spent several weeks in the hospital before being released from the service. His generation, growing up during the Depression, fighting in the Second World War, had learned lessons about work and sacrifice that so many in my generation did not face. He had become a survivor. More than that, he had discovered something important about the meaning of regular work and the dignity of life.

Dad taught me a lot about work when I was growing up, and the poverty we experienced taught me a lot about sacrifice. I remember how proud I felt when, after overhearing my mom talk about not having any food or money for supper, my brother and I combed the streets collecting pop bottles. We took them to the local grocery and cashed them in for the bologna we ate that night. Today it all seems a little unreal. Nevertheless, at the time I sensed that all of us had to sacrifice and that I was really contributing.

I also remember my first job. Old Lady Jackson, as we boys called her, had asked the pastor at the church if there were any "poor kids" who needed a summer job. He gave her my brother's name and address. My brother, Cameron, who was named after my father, was to go into ninth grade that fall. I was about to start the seventh. This white-haired "old lady" owned several rental properties—run-down frame houses and duplexes. For 25¢ an hour, I scraped the badly peeling paint off the walls, fighting legions of wasps in the 100° Texas heat. I tore down wallpaper, hung and plastered Sheetrock, and then painted both the outside and inside of her houses. I can still smell the cooking beans as the aroma came around from the other side of the worn duplex we were painting. And I can still see the ragged-looking kids and worn-out mom waiting for the truck-driver dad to pull up in his rig. By the middle of the summer, I was given a raise to 50¢ an hour, because she said that as far as she could tell, I was doing as much work as my brother, who had been hired for 50¢ an hour all along. The first things I bought with my wages were a pair of real walking shorts and a shirt. I can still see the brown shorts and the yellow plaid shirt. I was so proud not to be wearing someone else's cut-offs.

My dad helped me find my first real job, the kind that required a Social Security card. I was fifteen years old, and I needed regular employment. No, he did not get it for me, but he told me how to get it. He suggested that I try a restaurant named the Sirloin Stockade, managed by a Mr. Castleberry. Dad knew him and told me I should apply there for a job. I went in expecting to be hired on the spot, but to my surprise, he said he did not have any openings. I went home dejected and told my dad.

Dad said, "If you really want that job, you need to convince him that you are serious and not just some kid. You keep going back and asking him if he has any openings, and you will get a job some day." And so every week I would go into the restaurant and ask Mr. Castleberry if he had any openings. After six or seven weeks, and probably just to get me out of his hair, he hired me.

I went after it with a vengeance. Busing tables was not much fun, but I was very proud of my job and determined to prove to Mr. Castleberry that he had not made a mistake in giving me this chance. And I actually succeeded. I worked my way up the ranks from busboy to salad bar, and then all the way to grill man, in record speed.

I left Sirloin Stockade a year later for a job at the Whataburger down the street and 15¢ more per hour. A few years ago, my wife and I stopped into that Whataburger in Tyler, Texas, on the way home to Austin. The owner, S. A. Black, recognized me and refused to let us pay for our meal. He told my wife that I had been one of his best hands. My dad's remark about how proud he felt upon being told that he had made a hand in the oil fields echoed in my mind. Funny how proud I also was to be remembered as a "good hand."

There was a lot of personal sacrifice associated with the Whataburger job. Even though I needed the money, there were a lot of nights that I would rather have been with my friends or out on a date. I had to work six nights a week and was given only two weekend nights off a month. Nevertheless, I was beginning to have a more balanced perspective about life. I came to be just glad that I had a job. But there was still more to be learned. The paradox was that if I had not had that job, I might not have lived to write this book. One night, three of my best friends invited me to go out with them to a club where many young people gathered. I had to decline, to my great disappointment, for I had to work and could not get off. On their way, however, a tragic accident occurred, and only one returned alive. The disaster shook our close-knit community to the core. We were puzzled over the question of God's role in this tragedy. It was, of course, even more difficult for me. I had come so close to being in that car.

I believe that God is present in my life, and even in my work. It is, however, as mysterious as it is comforting. He does not ever give us guarantees. He often requires, instead, that we make painful sacrifices. There are, however, times when he shows us in the most subtle ways that he cares about these sacrifices, that he is involved in our work.

I have come to believe that God not only cares but actually uses our work in ways that are important to his purposes. Whether or not we enjoy the kind of job we have, he is still involved. There is a deep mystery here, but it is important for us. He saves us from feeling that our work doesn't count. I believe that God even cared for that scrawny little boy who pestered the tired restaurant manager about a job, and my burdened thirty-eight-year-old dad, who struggled with a heavy pipe in the oil patch, trying his best to take care of a wife and two kids still at home.

Remember this: God gave us Christ. He understands and values your sacrifice, too. He knows what our work demands; he is deeply aware of the sacrifice of self that all work entails. And when your work lets you down and you are discouraged, remember that he knows and he cares. He cared how I felt at the end of a hard day at Whataburger when I was exhausted, but also when I was able to pick up that blue paycheck to pay my school tuition and help with the rent. He cares.

# 11

# THE MYTH OF THE PERFECT JOB
## SETTING REALISTIC EXPECTATIONS

*Slaves, obey your earthly masters with fear and trembling, in sincerity of heart, as you obey Christ; not only while being watched, and in order to please them, but as slaves of Christ, doing the will of God from the heart. Render service with enthusiasm, as to the Lord and not to men and women, knowing that whatever good we do, we will receive the same again from the Lord, whether we are slaves or free.*

Ephesians 6:5-8

Have you ever felt that you were in the wrong job? Have you ever wondered if you would do it differently if you could start over? I recently met Doug Sherman, author of *Your Work Matters to God*, at a men's retreat. As the book suggests, he is involved in the ministry of God in the workplace. For a couple of days in the Texas Hill Country, approximately fifty of us dealt with gut-level questions concerning our lives as Christians in the business world—questions about leading and serving at the same time, questions concerning sensitive employee relations and tough management decisions.

A lot of us at the retreat were questioning whether we were in the right job, whether we had become stuck in the wrong profession. The questions often began with statements such as, "I'm not sure if being an accountant is really God's plan for my life," or "I'm bored, and I think that may be God's way of telling me I am not in the right job." They were asking the initiative type of question, and some struggled with the full-time ministry question. They wondered whether they had to go to seminary, become a pastor or missionary to be fulfilled, to feel certain that they were in tune with God's will for their lives.

The chances are that you have felt this way at some time in your life. In fact, it is almost endemic to men in this current generation, men in their thirties, forties, fifties, and even beyond. You may have seen some of the countless books written about discerning your gifts, getting the right job, maximizing your potential, and achieving career success. The talk shows and seminar circuits are filled with motivational, career counseling, "how to" programs, all promising a fresh start to a more fulfilling life.

Many of us are hurting inside about this. Almost every week some friend raises a question that lets you know that it constantly remains at the back of his mind. Do you remember Peggy Lee's old song "Is That All There Is?" It haunts me, for it seems to tell our story. It speaks of the initial excitement, and then the inevitable letdown as each of life's experiences is optimistically felt, enjoyed, then lost. The singer sighs after having experienced the excitement of her first fair—"Is that all there is? Is that all there is to the fair?" And as each stage of life is experienced, she keeps reflecting: "Is that all there is?" The painful conclusion in the chorus hits some of us where it hurts:

> If that's all there is, then let's keep dancing.

Our jobs, our achievements, our battles against competition, our struggles to make our quota, the pleasure in our promotions, and even the anxiety about downsizing and job loss— these are somehow just not enough, not enough to fill some nagging hurt deep inside. And yet it is hard to let go of the dream that a different job, the right job, could meet this need. So somewhere in the back recesses of our minds a small voice asks, "Is that all there is?"

Does being a Christian solve this? It hasn't yet solved it for most of my fellow Christians. It's not as easy as we've been told. In fact, being a Christian may complicate it further. All kinds of other questions come into play. What about the factor of God's will, God's plan, God's interaction in our lives as we struggle to be faithful stewards of God's gifts? Sometimes career changes are forced upon us by circumstances beyond our reach. Despite everything we can do, we are hit by layoffs, restructurings, cutbacks, bankruptcies, lawsuits—pressures we cannot control. Sometimes we try to see these as signs of God's special intervention in our lives. We desperately trust that they are part of some larger plan.

At other times, we wonder about taking the initiative. We wonder if our restlessness, our unsettling discontent is some kind of evidence that we haven't yet found God's master plan for our lives. We are troubled by questions: Should I go to seminary? Does God want me to teach? Can I really be a lawyer in this firm and be faithful to God's will? What of Paul's warning about being yoked with unbelievers? As Christians, it seems to get worse, not easier. Could God intentionally complicate these decisions for believers? Could he be saying, "I want you to struggle in the very area of your life in which you long to have peace"?

In my own struggle with career choices, I often have asked God to show me where he wants me. Should I stay put? Should I teach? Should I go back to school? More recently, however, I sense that I am coming to an even deeper peace. I have begun to wonder whether I have been asking the right questions. I have a hunch that God may be more interested in who I am, how I live my life, than in what title I have, what profession I practice.

Prior to that retreat, I had begun to wonder whether God was more concerned about me as a person. If this were the case, he would then, I surmised, want me to discover my true gifts. Once I did this, I thought, it would be simpler. The special use of my God-given gifts would then somehow confirm that I was in tune with God's will. Surely there is some truth to this.

Doug Sherman, however, approached the entire career choice question from a completely different angle. Without questioning the value of discovering God's gifts, Doug pointed out that job dissatisfaction today often results from a phenomenon unique to the last two generations. For most of our history, the majority of men did not have career choices. If dad was a farmer, you were likely to become a farmer, unless there wasn't enough land; then you moved on or went into the military. If dad was a cobbler, the chances are that you would become a cobbler. It is only now, when we are blessed with many more career options, that we feel such pressure to choose the right one, the perfect career.

Unfortunately, options for me can be a curse. Not only do I fear making the wrong choice, but I also feel a sense of loss for the options I didn't choose. I call this the Baskin Robbins Syndrome. The choice of one flavor, however sweet, raises the dilemma of thirty flavors unexperienced, some of which may have been better choices. We have often spent a lot of energy trying to decide among alternative paths.

Three of the insights Doug shared that weekend have stuck in my mind, and they have even begun to alter the way I view my work:

♦ 1. Work is not meant to be easy.
♦ 2. Excellence in my work is obedience to God.
♦ 3. Work is not God.

Most of us would quickly agree with the first. Even before the Fall, man was called to work. Genesis 2:15 says that the Garden of Eden was created first so that Adam could be put there "to till it and keep it."

Regardless of how you interpret the creation story, our entire history has consisted of work—work as hard labor, involving commitment and sacrifice. From this perspective, we realize that every job, like life itself, has its demands and rewards. Why should my work be different? How realistic is the expectation that work should be fun and fulfilling most of the time? Here's the bottom line question: Do the boredom of routine matters and the frustrations of bureaucratic hassles represent a nudge from God to do something else, or is it just part of what work inherently entails?

If work is hard, why is excellence in work important? Why does my work, not my title, matter to God? Doug talked about Paul's admonition to slaves, quoted from Ephesians at the beginning of this chapter. Their work often included such jobs as cleaning up after Roman orgies—not pleasant, not much opportunity for career satisfaction. Yet, and here is the point that is relevant to us, they were urged to do a good job. God calls all of us to do what is sometimes very painful and discouraging, sometimes personally humiliating. However, as long as we have that particular position, we are to accept the sacrifices involved.

As William E. Diehl points out to us in *The Monday Connection*, doing our duty and attempting to become as competent as possible are a large part of our responsibility as Christians. Diehl states that we must be competent in our work if we are to be effective in the workplace. Only after we achieve competency to do the job right, can we begin to ask, "Where is God in this situation?" Even the toughest job situations, to our surprise, will then involve opportunities to touch our world for God.

The most powerful insight I gleaned from that retreat was the realization that we often confuse God and work. Without realizing it, we sometimes demand attributes in our jobs that truly can come only from God. We want careers that promote self-actualization and give a sense of purpose, accomplishment, and good feelings. The right job is held up as the answer to our emptiness inside. Some of us have found ourselves moving from career to career, tasting, sampling, searching for more, for the perfect job. And all the while, we continue to be haunted by the nagging question, "Is that all there is?"

We certainly live in a society where job security is becoming a thing of the past, and job flexibility is the buzzword. We always need to reevaluate our gifts and consider our options. But I can see a little more clearly that I need to do a better job of accepting the nature of work and its inherent sacrifices. I need to accept some of the things I don't like and begin to see the service to God that my work entails. I want to be grateful that in my career struggles, I know that there is a God, that I can have a relationship here and now with Jesus Christ.

There is no perfect job. There never will be. What provides a new sense of balance and confidence, however, in even the toughest challenges, is recognizing that God may have a hidden purpose for me right here. And if that is all there is, just maybe it is enough.

# 12

# DAILY BREAD

## DETERMINING HOW MUCH IS ENOUGH

*"Lord, teach us to pray . . . ."*
*He said to them, "When you pray, say . . . :*
*Give us each day our daily bread."*

Luke 11:1*b*, 2*a*, 3

Daily bread—how much is enough? A tent? A tunic? A pair of sandals? A robe? An apartment? A house? A summer cottage? A Ford? A Lincoln? A BMW? A Mercedes? Social Security? An IRA? A company pension plan? $1,000,000 in CDs?

Give us each day our daily bread.

Dr. Tony Campolo spoke to a group of couples one evening in my hometown. He made the statement that he wasn't sure anyone could really consider himself or herself a Christian and drive a BMW. He based this on the theory that we Christians are called to live as Christ would have lived today. So the relevant question is, "Would Jesus buy a BMW?"

Dr. Campolo had nailed us. He was trying to get us to focus on our blessings and challenge us to become more generous to the poor. He may not really see the road to hell crowded with BMW-loving churchgoers, but he did make his point.

Dr. Campolo intended to wake us up, to enable us to see our own lives in light of God's commands. He was, in fact, challenging us to view our entire lives through the lens of Christian stewardship. He didn't want us to think of stewardship

74

just in terms of church pledges. He meant all of life! This hit hard.

It hit me because I have been able to accumulate some things, to provide for our family, and to earn a good income. But I grew up poor. Because we were Catholic, the parish priest in our small town let us go to the Catholic school for many years without paying tuition. Most of the kids in the school came from upper-middle-class families. I was aware that I did not dress as well as they did. My family did not do the things they did, did not have the things they had. So I felt inferior. And while this hurt, it also drove home a point. I became determined to be successful when I grew up. I thus set about the process of achieving success in worldly terms—college, law school, law-firm partner, marriage, children, nice home, civic accomplishments, church membership, societal acceptance—goals sought and attained. I had gotten there. But Dr. Campolo's speech left me wondering. I felt somehow put off balance by it.

Daily bread—how much is enough?

I went to an old family-owned department store in Austin one day just before it closed. It was open for the last time, having been bought out by one of the big national chains. My watch strap had broken and I needed a new one. There was a massive "Going Out of Business Sale"—everything 66⅔ percent off! Without meaning to, I started shopping. This was a bad sign, because normally I hate shopping. If the stores depended on me, they would go broke. I don't like to shop because I still don't trust my taste. Even after all these years, I still have the irrational fear that I will look stupid—like the poor kid in hand-me-down clothes bought from a thrift shop. Illogical! Maybe, but old feelings die hard. But this time I got caught up in the "feeding" frenzy. People all around me were saying, "Boy, these prices are incredible."

I found them incredible too! In fact, I soon found myself carrying two sweaters, two shirts, a pair of pajamas, and a coat. I asked a salesperson if I could set the stuff down somewhere while I went to get some more.

He looked blank and said, "There's no one to watch it." What could I do? I was desperate.

Then suddenly I thought, "What are you doing? Why are you buying this stuff? Yes, these are great prices—$10 for a $30 dress shirt; $12 for a sweater; $75 for a $225 coat. But do you really need any of this stuff? Did you think you needed it before you came in the store to buy a watch band? Why are you about to spend more than $250 on things you did not feel a need for thirty minutes ago?"

Now I was really confused. Great prices, great bargains, but the more I thought about it, the more uncomfortable I became. I stopped in my tracks. Here I was, in the midst of the crowd—people picking over tables of merchandise, inspecting and rejecting, arms overflowing. The scene resembled a giant ant hill. I started putting things back. Perhaps I would get only a few really great bargains. By the time I was finished, I had put everything back and walked out of the store without purchasing anything.

It was lunch time, and I was starved. I went to a take-out store and bought a sandwich. I needed something to restore my spirits after all that. As I sat at a sidewalk table eating, I thought about the idea of daily bread. It is obvious that in this country we have such abundance, such remarkable, incredible wealth. I sat there munching my sandwich, thinking of the pictures of people from television film clips, people lining up to buy their daily bread. The pictures of children with extended bellies and empty bowls, waiting for a ladle of food from a relief worker, came to mind. I thought of Dr. Campolo's feelings about the poor and about our responsibility to respond.

The next day, I went to the funeral of a friend's mother. She died with considerable wealth, and I knew that her children would inherit enough to provide a higher level of financial security than they had known before. How would it change them? Money cannot replace a mother, but I wondered what effect this would have on them over time.

I went for a run after the funeral. I needed time alone. As I was running, I kept thinking about daily bread and the Lord's Prayer. I thought of the Jews in the desert after they had escaped from Egypt—literally relying on God for their daily bread, manna, which could not be collected or stored up, but had to be harvested each day. I remembered a Sunday school lesson on the book of Ecclesiastes, in which the teacher reminded us that we cannot change the past; that the future is only a potential; that we must live today, for it is all we have.

At the end of her lesson, she said, "You know, even when we say the Lord's Prayer, we are allowed only to ask for our daily bread. We are not entitled to ask for enough surplus bread to last until retirement." So how are we supposed to save for our kids' college educations and contribute to a retirement plan? I needed a balanced perspective about this.

As I neared the end of my run, it occurred to me that God had answered the cries of the Hebrews in the desert. For in the Lord's Prayer, we are taught to pray collectively, as a people of God. Jesus did not tell us to say, "*My* Father who art in heaven." The prayer does not read, "Give *me* this day *my* daily bread." This was the scandal of it! The conclusion was not an easy one for me, but for the first time, I began to see the entire issue in a more communal light. There is enough wealth in this country, in this world, for everyone. No one really needs to go to bed hungry, to be without sufficient clothing. Admittedly, I was not entirely ready for this, but I saw that the problem does not lie in God's blessings, but in our collective stewardship of his gifts. It lies in a change of our will to see the issue in new ways. I work hard. So do you. I believe in everyone doing his own part. But Christ does not let it rest there.

The struggle for me has not ended. I am not prepared to sell all I have and become a missionary. Nor do I intend to never buy another shirt at a fine department store. But I do know that I need to continually remember my responsibility in the Body of Christ to serve my fellow humans, to seek to do God's will, and to remember Jesus' response to the plea, "Teach us to pray." To achieve the balance I need, I may need to seek his will about giving up some of the things that have, before I realized it, unbalanced my life. It may begin with this simple prayer: "Our Father, . . . Give us each day, our daily bread." Amen.

# 13

# WHAT DO MEN LIVE BY?
## MEETING OTHERS' NEEDS

*"Then the king will say to those at his right hand, 'Come, you that are blessed by my Father, inherit the kingdom prepared for you from the foundation of the world; for I was hungry and you gave me food, I was thirsty and you gave me something to drink, I was a stranger and you welcomed me, I was naked and you gave me clothing, I was sick and you took care of me, I was in prison and you visited me.' Then the righteous will answer him, 'Lord, when was it that we saw you hungry and gave you food, or thirsty and gave you something to drink? And when was it that we saw you a stranger and welcomed you, or naked and gave you clothing? And when was it that we saw you sick or in prison and visited you?' And the king will answer them, 'Truly I tell you, just as you did it to one of the least of these who are members of my family, you did it to me.'"*

Matthew 25:34-40

A friend of mine recently loaned me his copy of a short story titled "What Men Live By," by Leo Tolstoy. In the story, a poor Russian cobbler encounters a strange man who is naked and shivering in the cold. Moved to compassion, the cobbler and his wife, though they are desperately poor themselves, take the stranger in, feed him, clothe him, and give him a place to stay. They then even teach him to be a cobbler like themselves.

Later, a cruel rich man comes to the cobbler's house. He orders an expensive pair of boots, with strict instructions that the boots must last a full year or he will not pay for them. The stranger makes burial shoes instead of boots for the rich man. The next day, the rich man's son comes to the cobbler's house, asking for burial shoes instead of boots, because his father had died the night before.

Still later, a woman arrives with twin girls. She is seeking shoes, and she tells about adopting the twins after both their parents had died. Upon hearing her story, the stranger suddenly transforms himself into a radiant angel. He explains that earlier, as an angel, he had been sent to take the soul of the original mother of the twins to heaven. When he arrived at her deathbed, however, she begged to be able to live to take care of her twin daughters. The angel had compassion on her and disobeyed God. He returned to heaven without her soul to plead her case. It hadn't worked. God sent the angel, Michael, back to take the mother's soul and, when that was done, God had stripped off his wings and sent him back to earth, not to return to heaven until he had learned the answer to three questions: What is given to men? What is not given to men? What do men live by?

Michael explains that when the cobbler and his wife took him in, fed him, and clothed him, he learned the answer to the first question: "Love has been given to men to live in their hearts."

When the angel saw the hard rich man demanding boots that would last a year, he also saw the angel of death and knew that the rich man would die that night. And so the answer to the second question was revealed: "It is not given to men to know their own needs."

Then when Michael saw the woman with the twins and heard her story, he discovered the answer to the third question: "Man does not live by care for himself but by love for others." The angel had assumed that the twins would die without their mother, and yet, through the love of the kind woman, they had lived.

This short story intrigued me. The angel Michael had found a sort of balance. As I read it, I could not help thinking that most of us, like the rich man, live with fear and worry about what our needs may be tomorrow. I wonder how many of us are ordering the wrong pair of shoes at this moment.

Not long after I read that story, something happened to our family that seemed to be remarkably close to it. I was a chalice bearer for the service that Sunday, and so had to go to church early. My wife was bringing our ten-year-old son, Eric, later in our van. But as I looked out over the congregation in the church that day, I did not see Kay. After the service, we met at Sunday school. I asked her where she had been.

"Promise you won't get mad and I'll tell you," she teased.

"OK," I replied, wondering what could have caused her to detour at the last moment.

Then she told me the story. It seems she ran into a man on the sidewalk outside the emergency assistance offices next to the church. A lot of homeless people and panhandlers frequent this area because the church is in a downtown neighborhood. This man asked Kay if she knew when the offices would be open. There was something about the man that made my usually cautious wife feel the need to learn his problem. She did not know whether the offices would be open that day, Sunday. The man told her that he had lost his job at a local computer company, and his wife had been laid off by a department store. They had a baby a few months old, and they were now without a job or money. He was hoping to get some help until they could qualify for food stamps or until he could get another job. They did not even have diapers for the baby, and thus he had used his last clean T-shirt in that way.

As he spoke, my wife could see the bare apartment in her mind, the worried mother and fretful baby. Kay's heart cried out and, throwing caution to the wind, like the good Samaritan, she gathered the man into her van with our son Eric, and off they went to the store. She bought food, diapers, and other basic supplies. She took the man and the groceries to his apartment. She gave the items to his wife and held her hand and told her she would pray for them and that things would get better.

After she left the apartment, wide-eyed Eric asked, "How much did you spend, Mom?"

"About $75," she replied. "It should be enough to last them for a couple of weeks until they can get on food stamps."

"Gee, that's less than what we spent last week on my new tennis shoes," Eric remarked.

"That's right," Kay replied. It was a sobering moment.

"It's like this," Kay went on. "I am grateful that we have been able to buy especially nice shoes for you on occasion, but I am even more thankful that you and I could help these people."

I knew she had done the right thing, and I wondered what Eric had thought of his experience. Had he learned something about living by values that really count? Had he discovered that trying to meet the real needs of others may be even more important than his longed-for tennis shoes?

What do men live by? We who have been able to pay our bills and support our families have still another responsibility. We can't get away with just striving for personal financial stability. Even if we were to reach it someday, it could serve only to rot out the core of our souls. It could unbalance our entire lives. I know. I've seen it happen to friends. We all need to come to terms with the role of possessions in our lives. I do not have the inclination to become a monk, to give up all material things. I have already made major choices to be a husband and a father, and they compel me to search for ways to live in this world as a good steward of my resources. I have a duty to be prudent, to set up college funds for our children, to put money aside for retirement so that Kay and I will not be burdens to anyone.

I am expected to live by certain standards in my work and in our own community. I want my family to be comfortably housed. But I can't stop there. That isn't enough. I also have made additional choices. I have made a personal commitment to be accountable for the way I use these blessings. And so Kay and I will keep struggling and keep seeking God's guidance as we make the daily decisions this commitment requires. I have chosen to deal with the question, "What do men live by?" in ways that balance personal and social responsibilities. It is never easy. Risk and hard daily decisions are required. But this seems to be what God requires of all of us.

"Come, you that are blessed by my Father, inherit the kingdom prepared for you from the foundation of the world. . . ."

# 14

# WHAT WILL THEY SAY ABOUT ME WHEN I'M GONE?

## REFLECTING ON THE LIFE WELL-LIVED

*[B]ecause all must go to their eternal home; and the mourners will go about the streets . . . and the dust returns to the earth as it was, and the breath returns to God who gave it.*

Ecclesiastes 12:5*d*, 7

Great-aunt Myrtle died in the nursing home. Within a week, her third husband followed her. Two other husbands had left her twice widowed. Life had left her childless. One brother and one sister preceded her into the promised land. Another sister and various nieces, nephews, grand-nieces and -nephews, and great-grand-nieces and -nephews, as well as other relations, remained to remember her.

I loved Myrtle. She was the middle sister in a trio of grand southern dames. She was not really my aunt. She was my wife's great-aunt. Even so, she was my friend. She was one of the most real people I have ever known. If I close my eyes even now, I can see her so clearly—it is almost as if I could touch her, hear her voice, her musical laughter, see her mischievous smile, and remember her gentle teasing of her much more seriously inclined sisters. The triumvirate: Grandma Cora, Aunt Myrtle, and Aunt Mary.

They used to come to see us—to brighten our home with tales of adventure from times gone by. I remember them reliving for us the story of these three sisters and their younger "chaperone" brother driving to Colorado, alone, in the early 1900s, leaving the Normal School in Louisiana which the girls had attended, so that the oldest, Cora, could go on to college—almost unheard of at that time. Laughing and talking as each one tried to convince us that her particular version of events was the accurate one.

Myrtle loved to laugh and tease. I remember her playful taunts, like the time Myrtle, in the midst of her third marriage, teased long-widowed Mary and Cora: "Living alone—you know—without a man," Myrtle pontificated as the three ladies sat on our front porch rocking one spring evening. "Somehow, I just don't think it's natural."

Indignant, proper Mary retorted, "I buried my love!"

"I loved both of the two I buried," Myrtle replied, with a twinkle in her eye.

And then there was the time Myrtle told about the nosy hair stylist in the beauty parlor. Apparently this woman was "man hungry" and desperate to get married. She could not fathom how Myrtle had managed to marry for the third time.

"Come on, Myrtle—tell me. What's your secret?" the stylist entreated.

"I'll never tell you my secret," Myrtle chuckled as she clicked her tongue against the inside of her front teeth. Then she explained, "I don't ever know when I may need it again!"

Full of life, ready to move on, leading her own life, eccentric, elastic, fun to be around, full of surprise and opinion—that was Myrtle. She refused to fly because she had worked for years in an airplane manufacturing plant.

"Fly? Not me. I know what really goes on in there. Why, I could tell you stories that would curl your toes!" she liked to exclaim as we brought her to our home from the Greyhound bus station.

She lived frugally and had saved quite a tidy sum over the years. Thus she enjoyed a relatively independent air. I don't remember ever hearing her complain. Oh, she fought her battles, had her friends and her enemies at work and in life. She had her favorite restaurant—Luby's Cafeteria—where the coffee refills were free and the food "not too spicy." What I want to say is that she was just so real to me. She enjoyed being who she was, and she conveyed an honest sense about life. Without her saying so directly, she had a deep, abiding faith in God, and a lighthearted joy in people resulted from it.

And she had died. Our family went to the funeral. It was a hot day. The crowd was small. It had been a while since she had been physically able to attend church. Not many in the congregation knew her—another older member from the nursing home. The minister was young and new and did not know Myrtle at all.

We drove in the funeral procession to the cemetery where the service was to be held. The day was hot, muggy.

I spoke to the minister. "Did you know Myrtle?"

"No, I'm sorry to say, I didn't. But I understand that she was sick for a long while, and she had a hard life."

"NO!" I wanted to scream. "That isn't enough. There is so much more!"

Isn't there more that could be said about this life, this all too real human being that we had loved so much? My heart sank with the thought that all the minister could say was that she had died after a long sickness and had lived a hard life. The injustice overwhelmed me. So I pulled the minister aside.

I said, "Let me tell you about Myrtle."

I told him about the woman I had known, about her sense of humor, about her basic commitments and values, about the love she had for her family, about her life as supportive sister, aunt, and friend. Perhaps others could have done it better. After all, I had only known her for a few years. But she had established a unique place in my heart. She had been direct, independent, and joyful, and in our world today these traits are all the more valuable. I was determined that some of those special things that made us love her so much be remembered by this well-meaning young minister as he tried to do justice to this great lady's life.

He gave a good eulogy. He even thanked me indirectly as "one of her relatives" who had filled in the details about her life. Afterward, I was so grateful that I had taken the moment to talk with him. I felt that I had paid my respects to her in a personal way—if only because I had valued her and loved her as my special friend.

But there is more to this incident. Myrtle's funeral had touched a nerve. It had prompted me to wonder how I want to be remembered—what I hope will be said about me, about a life well-lived.

During the next year, I returned to this question again and again. In part, I think our lives will be measured by the things we have done, the places we have gone, and the experiences we have had. But there is more to it. Our lives really will be remembered by the character of our commitments, the integrity of our relationships, and our unselfish concern for the good of others. A senior lawyer in my first law firm, when I was just a young attorney, advised me never to forget old friends and never to be afraid to make new friends. That is a start. I believed this to be wise advice, and I have tried to take it to heart. But I want even this advice to be balanced by the authentic, spirited, unselfish things I have seen in the life of Aunt Myrtle.

When I die, what do I want them to say? I decided to make a list, a kind of litany of some of the things that are beginning to seem important to me today, in the middle of my life. Of course it will change as time goes on. However, writing this out was a useful, if somewhat unnerving, exercise. It helped me to see myself through the eyes of others, to take an accounting of where I might be at the end of the road. You might try it, for it provides a unique sense of perspective and balance.


## EULOGY ON THE DEATH OF MARTIN CAMP

He loved and trusted in God as the One who directed his life.

He earnestly tried to do what is right—acknowledging his failures and moving on beyond them to try again.

He was grateful and hopeful in difficult times.

He was a good husband and a good father.

His friends trusted him and depended upon him.

LIFE ON THE HIGH WIRE

He gave the gift of humor and laughter to others, even in
the midst of tears.

He knew that all he had was a trust from God and was
therefore generous and unselfish with time and possessions.

People from all walks of life called him a friend.

He was careful in his work, a good and conscientious counselor with his clients, and a loyal, helpful colleague.

He reached out to be a good steward of God's gift of life, to
follow the call of his Savior, and to serve him in simple
faith.

May he rest in peace.


What do you want them to say about you when you are gone?

# 15

# WHOSE LIFE AM I LIVING?
## BECOMING YOUR OWN MAN

*"A wise child makes a glad father."*
Proverbs 15:20a

*"Am I now seeking human approval, or God's approval? Or am I trying to please people? If I were still pleasing people, I whould not be a servant of Christ."*

Galatians 1:10

I recently attended a seminar on succeeding in business. During one of the workshops, we dealt with the topic of communication. My task was to listen to the person seated on my left and enable him to share something that had meant a great deal to him—something that had given him a great deal of pride.

He was middle-aged, a businessman from a nearby city. When I asked him about his achievements, he told a fascinating story. His father had been an enthusiastic pilot in the air force and had gone on to become a flight instructor. There was nothing he had enjoyed more than getting the young pilots up in the air and snapping orders at them. He had spent hours at it every day.

It was no surprise that my new friend grew up with a deep longing to fly. His dream was to become a pilot like his dad. However, he ran up against a tremendous problem: He couldn't pass the physical for flight training! He had joined the ROTC in college, hoping to graduate and be accepted for further training as an air force pilot, but the medical examination uncovered a preexisting condition. It wasn't bad, but it was enough to keep him from flying.

He was bitterly disappointed, but he went on with his life. He served his time in the service, went into business, and became a reasonable success. Even so, through the years he felt that he had failed in his father's eyes because he could not fly—could not share in the one thing that was most important to his father.

Eventually, he decided to take flying lessons. One day shortly after he received his pilot's license, he took his dad for what was supposed to be a country drive. Instead, they drove to the local airport. He checked out a plane and took his father up for a flight. At last he was able to fly with his father! His dad was so excited that he began to bark orders at his son, just as he had in the old days when he had taught the young fighter pilots. My new friend's eyes sparkled with pride as he related this story.

In response to my question, "Do you still fly?" he replied, "No, I gave it up a few years ago. It takes too much time, and it's an expensive habit." That seemed strange to me, but I could not bring myself to ask the question burning in my consciousness: "Is your father still alive?" For some reason, I felt that his decision to stop flying might have corresponded with the death of his father. I wondered to myself, If flying had really been such a passion in his life, would he have given it up?

When the group reconvened, each participant told about the accomplishment of which he was most proud. It seemed to me that, again and again, the accomplishments were related to parental expectations. One man in his sixties told of dropping out of school, getting into trouble with the law, and being sent to the army instead of jail. He later got his GED and bachelor's degree and passed the CPA exam with the highest grade in his state. Why was this the most important event in his life? Because he had proved to his parents that he was not a "washout." Another told of taking over the family business and carrying on what his father had started so many years ago.

*Wow,* I said to myself, *what is going on here?* I began to review my own choices in life. They were not as clear-cut as I had thought. I had worked hard, paid many of my own bills in high school and college, had a good record in college, and won a handsome scholarship to law school. I was successful. Or was I? How much of this really could be said to be my own choice? Was I a success personally, or had I been driven by parental pressures that I had not consciously recognized?

Other questions came to mind, leaving me with a sense of being caught a little off balance. How much do I let my parents' or society's or my friends' expectations and values govern my decisions? What kind of car should a lawyer drive—or, for that matter, an accountant, a plumber, a computer programmer, a coach? Where should I live? What clothes should I wear? What message am I sending to my family and to the world by my choices? I had thought that I was an independent type, but now I began to wonder.

As I thought more about this, I asked myself just how many of my decisions had been influenced primarily by the expectations of others, their perceptions of who I should be and how I should live my life. I knew that if I were honest, I would have to admit that trying to meet others' expectations had consumed a large amount of my energies over the years. And I was certain that I was not alone in this preoccupation with what Paul calls trying to please people rather than God. One thing began to come clear: Unless I found out who or what was the driving force in my life, I would never succeed in becoming my own man.

On the way home from the meeting, another thought occurred to me: I am supposed to be a Christian, but I had left God out of these questions. Just how did my understanding of God influence the answer to the question of the driving force in my life? Did I see him as God the Father, the giver of the Ten Commandments, sitting on the Seat of Judgment? Did I see him as the Christ, sitting at the dinner table with the drunkards and prostitutes, the tax collectors and sinners, offering me eternal life if only I believed and accepted Jesus as my Lord and Savior? Or did I see God as the Holy Spirit, empowering me to improve my life, encouraging me to make the changes that might lie ahead, enabling me to struggle with my sins?

I realized that at different times in my life, I have thought of

God in each of these ways and, I am sure, in many, many more. It all boiled down to one question: Whose life was I living? My own? God's? Or someone else's? Sure, I could profess then and now that I have given my life to Christ, that I have made him the Lord of my life, but whose life am I really living *today?*

As the question simmered in my mind, I remembered reading William Barclay's commentary on Matthew 8:21-22, in which someone asks to be able to bury his father before following Jesus. Jesus responds, "Follow me, and let the dead bury their dead." This passage sounds harsh, almost inhuman. But yet, I wondered, could it provide some help?

Barclay surmises that if we understand the culture of the time, the language usage, and the dynamics of what probably was going on in that setting, we could interpret the plea of this potential disciple as meaning, "When my father has died and I have fulfilled all my duties to him and my family, and I am free to choose my own life, then I will follow you." Viewed from this perspective, it is much easier to see that Jesus is admonishing the young man to seize the moment, to follow now, to live his own life, even if there are unpleasant consequences such as parental disapproval.

Whose life am I living? How do I judge success in my life? Whom am I trying to please? These questions lie buried somewhere in our subconscious, influencing our actions and feelings about ourselves.

I like Barclay's comments. They encourage me to go forward to live my own life. They tell me that the Lord has a place for me that no one else can fill or even understand. As long as it fits in with his teachings and my responsibility to love others, why not live my own life, become my own man?

Here is the clincher: No one but the Lord can understand me as deeply or value me as profoundly or call me to be my best. Talk about balance. Talk about a sense of satisfaction. I can't imagine anything greater. And talk about a challenge. God gives *me* a special purpose. He wants me to become my own man.

As I pulled off the main road and onto the familiar road leading to our house, I realized that I had made some kind of subtle choice. I would expose all my past decisions to God. I would do it in some fresh way I hadn't tried before. I would ask him for help. I would let the "dead bury the dead." And now I would be not only my own man, but something more—*his* own man.

# 16

# MY DAD IS A WORKAHOLIC
## TAKING CHARGE OF YOUR LIFE

*You remember our labor and toil, brothers and sisters; we worked night and day, so that we might not burden any of you while we proclaimed to you the gospel of God.*

1 Thessalonians 2:9

He was a junior in high school, bright, athletic, good looking, an all-American kid. We had met at the health club at the Four Seasons Hotel. The previous Friday, just as I was wrapping up the week, I had consented to draft an agreement with a Monday deadline. It meant returning to the office after church and spending a long Sunday afternoon. I decided to get some exercise before tackling the assignment, so I went to work out.

He told me that he and his sister and their mom had come to spend the weekend, just to relax before he started back to school. His tone and phrasing led me to assume that either his parents were divorced or his father had died. He went on to say that he and his mom and sister really liked to come to Austin, to this particular hotel, just to get away.

We talked about what it was like to be in high school. He said he wanted to do well, to make good grades so he could go to a good college and have the chance for a good job. He explained that while he used to play every sport, now he had decided to limit his athletics to football, basketball, and track. After all, one has to accept limits, make choices! I told him that my older son also enjoyed sports, that he in fact wanted to be a professional baseball player. I also acknowledged that while such a dream would be difficult to achieve, I was sure that without such dreams, no one ever succeeded in becoming a professional athlete.

He asked me about being a lawyer. Was it a good job? I said that I certainly enjoyed it. I had found a lot of freedom in it. As he continued to question me about it, I wondered where all this was going. Suddenly, he abruptly changed the subject and announced that his dad was a banker. He worked for a large bank. I was slightly startled—this child's father was not dead, his parents were not divorced. We then talked about playing golf, and he commented that his parents were going to join a country club.

"Does your dad play golf?" I asked.

"No," he answered. "Dad grew up in a small town. He doesn't play golf or tennis. In fact, he doesn't do much of anything except work. My dad is a workaholic." He had been talking my ear off. I think I was beginning to understand why.

I found myself defending his dad. I talked about how hard the banking business had become, how competitive it was, with so many banks being closed or consolidated, so many people losing their jobs. I told him I was sure it was rough for his dad right now. He did not respond. He didn't quit talking, but he changed the subject. We talked until I had to go, but after I returned to my office, his words kept ringing in my ears: "My dad is a workaholic."

Why are so many of us men called workaholics? "Addicted to work" is the denotation that the suffix "-aholic" implies; it means someone who can't stop working, is compulsive in this behavior. It's not a compliment. People ask, Where does dedication stop and addiction begin? I wondered if his dad was really working because he was afraid he would lose his job, if the competition at the bank was so fierce. Who knows. I had a good idea, however, that if he had tried to explain this to his family, he would have hit a dead end. Here I was on Sunday afternoon, and the explanation had not been easy. How many of us hear ourselves trying to explain our work demands to our wife and children? We say that this present sacrifice is required for the good of the family, that we have to respond to forces beyond our control. Maybe so. But sometimes, let's admit it: Resolving work problems comes a lot easier than trying to regain control of our family life at home.

Give the man a break, I thought. What if he did have family tensions? What if his job brought him the only satisfaction in his life? Was he escaping a wife, a home, a marriage that he no longer wanted or felt capable of dealing with? Did he have a host of unmet expectations about himself that only work could fulfill, perhaps a dad of his own to compete with, some driving sense of insecurity to overcome? Theories of "pop psychology" ran rampant in my head.

What about his son? Disciplined, hardworking, family-oriented. Somewhere he learned that you need to make choices, that you have to work for the things that are important to you. Had he learned these things from this dad, this father that he called a workaholic? When he used the word, he did not say it in a particularly derogatory way; he was very matter-of-fact—like someone describing an automobile. But there was an obvious emptiness in his tone. I wondered, too, how my children would describe me. Would they use the word *workaholic*?

As I recalled again, the apostle Paul stressed the value of work. As tentmaker, he toiled "night and day" in order not to be a burden to the churches he shepherded. But, just as his Master was not a workaholic and took time to be with and enjoy those he loved and to be alone with the Father, Paul no doubt knew something about balance. True, he probably did not have a lot of leisure time in his dual-career journey. I wondered how he did it.

Other dedicated men came to mind. Here in Kuwait, a full-time dental surgeon also serves as a voluntary pastor to his parish. He is an ordained minister as well as a dentist. His wife is a doctor, and they have two sons. So how does a man do it all? How does he put in overtime at his work, spend so-called quality time with his family, and be active in his church and commu-

nity? How does he grow as a human being in the midst of all
this? Where does the concept of self-sacrifice fit in?

Remember the song "Cat's in the Cradle"? A couple of lines
went like this:

> When are you coming home, Dad?
> I don't know when, but we'll get together then, son.

I never think of these words without the haunting thought—
do my children hear me reply to them this way? The song then
reverses the problem. When the father retires, the shoe is on the
other foot. He discovers too late that his son has no time for his
retired dad, just as the dad had no time for his growing son. A
grim fate it is: "the sins of the father" indeed!

What is "quality time," anyway? Does it have to do with activities? Sometimes I feel that men are judged primarily on the num-
ber of baseball games coached and recitals attended. I believe we
may have let the pendulum swing too far. Our children become
involved in a schedule of activities that would exhaust an
Olympian. Single parents and two-career parents often find themselves overwhelmed. At the same time, they are rent with guilt if
they can't afford the time or money for a child to play on a team
or attend the fourth birthday party that month (bearing just the
right present, of course).

Here is where you and I have to get tough. We actually have
more potential, more strength, even more virtue, in the old-fash-
ioned sense of that word, than we realize. We must get tough to
push back some of the other demands placed on us. We must
get tough in order to say, "Activities aren't really enough. I want
to get to know my wife and kids."

We have all heard of "tough love." The problem is that it usually isn't tough enough. What I'm talking about is reasserting
our natural desires to communicate with our families, becoming
"tough enough" to care. By showing honest example, by sharing
our hurts and struggles, by putting our time into really building
a family—by doing all this in today's world, we show our real
strength. All too often we are not ready to face the emotional

issues. We make too many choices based on avoiding the potential for family conflict or to satisfy some work-related ego need. The real danger, however, lurks in avoiding the honest communication with our families, trying to postpone the pain. When we do that, we also postpone, maybe forever, the potential of joy.

As a father, I realize that I am teaching my sons and daughter daily by the way I live my life. Talking to that all-American boy at the health club reminded me that I need to include my children (and my wife) in my work life. I need to share with them what it means to be a lawyer, why I work, and what I do. I also know that I need to keep asking myself why I work, and where my work fits into my life and the lives of those most dear to me.

I have come to realize that it is up to me to maintain a very delicate balance between my work and my other roles. My work affects many other things in my life. If I do not feel good about my work, it influences the way I relate to my wife and children. More of us than we realize become unfaithful to our families when our work goes sour. Thus, being successful at work is important to me. But to allow this work-drive, whatever its inner motivation, to take over my life would be a disaster. It would impact my wife and children.

So what can I do? What should I do to try to find some balance? I asked myself this until one day I decided to grow up as a husband and father, as a man, and take some responsibility. I stopped asking, "What are you doing? Why are you doing it? What result do you want to achieve?" and I took charge of my life again. If I see that I am putting work ahead of family for some nonessential reason, such as my ego or to avoid a situation at home, I will pluck out the problem as if I were pulling out a weed. Problems avoided simply grow. I decided that my work will not become a refuge from my other responsibilities.

But what if the conflict is real? What if it looks as if I am on my way to being a workaholic in the eyes of my family? Sure, I can try to compromise. Is the Monday deadline really a deadline? Can I postpone the trip? Can someone else do it? Can I reject Friday's obligation and avoid the Sunday office trip?

Suppose the conflict can't be avoided. The boss says "go." So share the pain. Explain it to those it affects. Make up for it, and *really* make up for it. Show the family that you really missed them. The critical issue is to communicate fully and make up for it doubly. Just because they understand doesn't mean they won't be disappointed. You know what this means—you must become the parent in truth. I have made a decision: I will not disappoint those I love!

One exercise that works is to ask: How will I feel about this decision in five years? What impact will this choice have on my wife and children? This single question puts most things into perspective, and it also helps provide great motivation.

And I have found that when I really show clients and fellow workers that my God and my family come first, they not only respect this, but they often help me carry out these responsibilities. I had to honestly face the fact that sometimes I have sacrificed faith and family. Then I decided to accept the responsibility and change.

In the final analysis, there are no easy answers. I will struggle to maintain this balance as long as I live. To live deeply and successfully, I must deal with this, accept responsibility for it, and be tough enough to handle it. All of us must accept this: The struggle is better than the surrender. God is in this with us, and so I pray to him that I will be a good father to my children and a good husband to my wife, taking comfort that Jesus the carpenter understands the meaning of work in my life.

# 17

## My Father, My Friend
### SEEING YOURSELF IN THE EYES OF YOUR FATHER

*Be wise, my child, and make my heart glad.*
Proverbs 27:11

How did you make it through all these years, Dad? All the really bad times? Whom did you talk to, confide in? Did you have any really close friends to rely on?"

I asked my father these questions a couple of years ago. I had been reflecting upon his life—how, like so many of his generation, he had experienced what seemed to me much greater hardships than my generation has faced. The son of an alcoholic father, he had grown up in the Depression, dirt poor. In the ninth grade, he had dropped out of school to support his family—his mom and two younger brothers. As I have noted earlier, he married at the ripe old age of seventeen. By the following year he was a father and a Marine, soon to be injured at Guadalcanal in World War II. In his late thirties, he lost his business, went bankrupt, started over. At forty-six, his wife, my mother, committed suicide. As we were speaking, he was in his late sixties and fourth marriage. He was more tenacious than any man I had ever met. He was and remains a survivor.

But where did this strength come from? I frankly had no idea. Where were his friends and supporters? I wanted to know. I honestly did not recall Dad talking much about friends. The people around him had always been customers and co-workers—names I had heard over the years. But not much real talk about friends, fishing buddies, or golf pals. Dad did not do those things. He worked almost all the time.

Dad's answer surprised me: "Friends, someone I could really talk to? Well, there were times when I tried to talk to the priests, you know, in the blackest times, but honestly, they did not really know me and I did not really think they understood. Other than the boys in the foxholes in WWII, I did not have any really good friends. I certainly didn't have a best friend, someone I could really talk to—that is, other than you."

"Me, why me?" I wanted to shout. "I'm not a friend, I'm your son, and you're my dad. You're supposed to be the strong one, the wise one, the one I turn to in times of need." As all these emotions began to well up inside me, I realized that, even as Dad was paying me a supreme compliment, I was not ready to hear it. It was true that over the years we had had that kind of relationship. Dad had talked freely to me about almost everything going on in his life. He had not tried to hide his warts or project some image of perfection. And often I had been there for him, both emotionally and financially. Nevertheless, there was still a part of me, deep inside, that had always wanted a different relationship. It had been there all those years, a part that wanted someone to understand me, to provide the emotional and financial support that *I* had needed. Perhaps it had been some idealized version of a "Father Knows Best"-type character. I'm not sure, but I think I wanted someone on a pedestal—but not just a "friend," even a best friend.

I did not discuss my feelings with my dad at that time. The conversation moved on to other topics. But I have thought a lot about his remark since then. It had been a compliment, but it also had been something else. I wasn't exactly sure. I know that I wondered what kind of person I would have been if I had a different dad, one who had been able to be there in a different way. The more I thought about it, the more I have realized that I am so intertwined with my father that I cannot answer this question. I do not know how I would have turned out. Too much has happened. But I do suspect that those early struggles provided the context in which I had to become self-reliant. My sister and brother had similar experiences. We had to learn how to take care of ourselves. The irony is that if you measure a parent's success by the outcome of his children, Dad would have won a prize. What it basically says, however, is that your background won't stop you. You can overcome almost any obstacle.

Over the years, I came to recognize that Dad had given me many things that don't have a price tag. He probably gave me more than I had understood at the time. He repeatedly told me that I had a certain spark, that I could do whatever I set out to do. His expectations were high, and I struggled to meet them. There were, however, also times when he let me fail. He did not always reach in with money or influence. I learned that I had to rely on myself. He told me that I should learn to be true to myself, that I should accept myself as I was. This was strong medicine for an adolescent. He also taught us that sometimes bad things would happen. Even so, we would survive.

"This too shall pass" was his motto whenever times were tough. It provided a kind of balance for our lives. This inherent wisdom seems to be passing down, for our oldest son has now adopted it. He seems to have his grandfather's sense of tenacity and poise. Dad told me that every man has some kind of problem, a tiger on his back that he just has to accept and overcome. In this, we are all like Paul with the thorn in his side. Dad's gifts were those of one friend to another, whether he realized it or not. What he gave, however, had value measured in character, not coin. But here is an interesting point. He was far from perfect. And he made many mistakes. So have you and I. But perfection may not be that important.

The relationship between fathers and sons is very complex. There is an inherent element of competition in most such relationships. History is replete with kings deposed by their sons. It happened in 1995 in the small Persian Gulf state of Qatar. As I write this, the deposed king, the father, is living in exile, vowing to return to his throne. And the reigning king, the son, is calling for assistance to support him after an unsuccessful coup by those loyal to the former monarch.

As I think about this matter of fathers and sons, I remember other stories from the lives of my friends. One grew up in a well-to-do home, but suffered several financial setbacks as he tried to make his own mark in the world.

One day at breakfast he confided, "You know, I really can't complain about anything about my father. He has always been a model father. He is a successful doctor who provided everything we could want. He was always there for me. He went to the ball games and set aside time for me. Perfect—that is what he was. And yet, I don't really know how to say this, except that it is really hard being his son. I feel such pressure to be like him. I don't think I can. I won't be as successful as he is. Look at me now, with these financial problems. No matter how hard I try, I will always be in his shadow."

I did not know what to say to this friend, but I knew his pain was real. Perfection doesn't always work.

I also thought of the other side of this coin, of a friend who talked one day about his dismay with his kids. My friend was one of the pillars of the community, financially successful, devoted to church and community service. There probably was not a title, position, or honor he had not received. He also had a beautiful family with two grown children. I admired him for what he had accomplished in life. However, he explained that he had grown up poor, the oldest son of an unsuccessful father. As a result, he had vowed to provide everything for his family that he had lacked as a child: stability, prosperity, options. And he had done it. But strange results had recently appeared. His daughter had complained to him that she did not think she would ever find a husband as good as he is. His kindness and his provisions had seemed to backfire. His son seemed to have somewhat similar problems. He had no ambition, no desire to get ahead financially, and he told an exasperated father that he knew he could never achieve what his father had, and so he did not want to try.

"Now let me ask you, what have I accomplished?" my friend moaned. "I've tried to be this perfect dad, and now my kids have inferiority complexes. It's just too ironic. And I really do not know what I am supposed to do about it." How perfect is perfection, after all? How balanced does it leave you?

Now it comes close to home. Was I, in reaction to my childhood, trying to be that perfect father too? Was I trying to do more than I should? And how would it affect our children? Is there a balance between absence and indulgence?

Oddly enough, Dad was right. We had grown up as friends. He had needed me, and I had needed him. It was honest. That was the key. And it had worked.

"Make 'em independent." That is Dad's current advice. "Look at you and your brother and sister. You guys came out all right. Help them as you can, but remember, there's nothing wrong with a little hard work either."

My father, my friend. Even in his more unbalanced times, he could give a gift of balance and independence to me. His honesty about himself and his shortcomings still help me accept myself. He was not perfect, and neither am I; and I should not expect perfection in our children. As I think now about my father and our relationship, I realize that in spite of everything, his wisdom was sound. As dads today, it is so easy to get discouraged. Big mistakes occur, but so what? The wisdom of our heavenly Father, which Dad somehow had picked up, is that any of us can try again. That is the meaning of grace, and it is real.

# 18

# KNOWLEDGE IS POWER
## RECOGNIZING YOUR NEED FOR FRIENDS AND INTIMACY

*He who forgives an offense fosters friendship,*
*but he who dwells on disputes will alienate a friend.*
*A rebuke strikes deeper into a discerning person*
*than a hundred blows into a fool.*

Proverbs 17:9-10

I was having lunch recently with a new friend whose life, on the surface, seems very different from mine. I am married, with three children and a long list of commitments that seem to fill my time and energy every day. Sometimes these obligations admittedly get a little too heavy. They take up more time than they should, and I feel as if I were flying on automatic pilot. On the other hand, my friend is single, lives alone, and has a job that allows him to leave at a regular time each day. He usually even has weekends free. This past weekend, for instance, he and a friend spent hours learning how to use rented RollerBlades.

Let's face it, this does have appeal. I asked my friend if he enjoyed living alone, being by himself, answerable to nobody. Sounded interesting, perhaps even a little too interesting. Frankly, there was never a time in my life when I wasn't either a student or a married man. I had been your basic ambitious youth, conforming to the mainstream American dream of family, house, cars, and career. Then I had married, and a family had come along. It was what I had wanted, but still, I wondered . . .

My friend responded that yes, he did enjoy being alone. He

not only valued the time to himself, but in fact, needed it. He went on to say that he always had been independent, had learned to rely on himself to meet his needs. It wasn't that he didn't enjoy other people; he liked doing things with friends. But basically, he did not like to depend upon others. And then he made a statement that struck me as quite personal: Other people can let you down, hurt you. He said he did not like to experience pain.

I was interested in his answer, so I asked if he were truly close to anyone. He replied that he was close to his parents, but not really to anyone else, and he intentionally kept it that way. It was the coldest statement I had ever heard. He added that to him, knowledge was power, and the fewer people who really knew him, the fewer would have power over him, the power to hurt him: no vulnerability; no pain.

I asked, "What do you do when you are alone? How do you spend that time?"

He responded that he loves to read. In fact, he was currently reading a philosophy book titled *From Socrates to Sartre.* He also said he likes to watch television, and if he were bored, he could always call up a friend and go out. As he was speaking, the words of the poet John Donne, which Paul Simon had built into a folk classic, came to mind: "No man is an island." I told my friend that he sounded like the man in Paul Simon's song, who claimed that his books were all he needed, that he avoided friendship and was really like a rock that felt no pain.

My friend laughed and said, "Hey, I'm not that bad. I have friends; I'm not a hermit. I just don't let many people get too close to me. I'm a private person." I don't know. Was he actually paraphrasing Paul Simon's song in talking about himself? It sounded too neat.

All afternoon following our lunch, I wondered about his apparent balance of privacy and power. Was he really able to keep a sense of balance by such hard-core privacy? Could any of us? Did I need more privacy in my life? I thought about the power of even knowing a person's name. You call out, "Hey you!" and you may get a response. But almost everyone responds when you call them by name. It is as simple as that. If someone remembers my name, it affects me. And if it is true about just knowing my name, what would it mean if someone knew even more about me? Surely it is true that the more someone knows about me, the more power he or she has to hurt or to uplift me, to cause pain or joy, to betray or support. Is friendship inevitably going to cause us pain, to unsettle us, to unbalance, rather than support our lives? Was the unknown author of the proverb right when he said that a good friend has much more influence over me than a host of enemies or mere acquaintances? Should we then avoid good friends?

The story of the Samaritan woman in the Gospel of John underscores this point at first. But then it reveals more; when Jesus initially asks for a drink, she questions why he, being a Jew, would associate with her, a woman and a Samaritan. She knows a little about him.

Then Jesus replies, "If you knew the gift of God, and who it is that is saying to you, 'Give me a drink,' you would have asked him, and he would have given you living water" (John 4:10). Knowledge, when it concerns Jesus, could bring much more: He explains to her that this personal relationship would be like eternally flowing water. It would never run out.

This relationship would also contain the most intimate truth. Jesus reveals just how much he knows about the woman by asking her to go and bring her husband. When she replies that she has no husband, Jesus amazes her by revealing that he knows that she has had five husbands and is not married to the man she is now living with. Knowledge is power, yes, but in relationship with Jesus, it becomes a different kind of power—an intimate truth that heals, a truth that restores perspective, and therefore balance.

There is, however, still more to this incident. Immediately after Jesus reveals that he knew her adulterous past, she replies that she recognized something about him: "Sir, I see that you are a prophet."

Later, she tells her neighbor about Jesus: "Come and see a man who told me everything I have ever done. He cannot be the

Messiah, can he?" Her curiosity then becomes contagious. John continues that many believed because of what the woman said, and still more believed after they had met Jesus and spent time with him.

"They said to the woman, 'It is no longer because of what you said that we believe, for we have heard for ourselves, and we know that this is truly the Savior of the world.' " From her initially superficial relationship with Jesus grew an in-depth knowledge of his healing power—not only for her but for many others.

Perhaps you have become caught by the lure of personal independence. The more I listened to my single friend, the more intriguing it sounded. Individualism is a powerful force in our society today. Self-reliance, self-actualization, doing your own thing, is in vogue. I read that over 25 percent of us live alone. Stores now stock single servings of all kinds of prepackaged food. A travel article extols the advantages of traveling alone. We are sucked into this promise because we have been hurt, and we want to avoid being hurt again.

My friend never admitted it, but I guessed that deep hurt lay behind that brave nonsense. Sure, friendship can lead to pain. You finally give in and let yourself grow close. You trust. You open up. You tell someone your hurts. Then he spills the beans. And you die a thousand deaths. Okay, my friend's defense mechanism of keeping his distance to avoid pain is one way of dealing with this dilemma: no trust; no pain.

There is only one problem with this isolation: It hurts! Loneliness is even more painful than betrayal. We are caught in the dilemma of being human. We trust, and we may be hurt. We isolate ourselves from in-depth, shared-knowledge relationships, and we hurt even more! Potential hurt and love are deeply joined.

If there are no people in our lives who know us well enough to cause us pain, then they won't be there to bring us joy. They won't be there to rejoice with us when good things happen or hold us up when hurts appear. Even more important, they won't be there to set us straight when we start down a wrong path, or to help us realize when we are wrong. Lack of intimacy may provide some protection, but there is a price.

I am not suggesting that we should bare our souls to anyone who is willing to listen. But I know that there is a unique, special power in forming relationships with a few others in which honesty and sharing can take place. It is one of our primary strengths for restoring our balance when we have been badly shaken.

Balance is not an individual achievement. Trust takes time and commitment, but the rewards are great. A sense of community sustained the early church as it met in homes, as the people prayed, praised God, and shared their lives together. In the past few years, I have sought out both individuals and small groups of committed Christians, with whom I have been able to be honest, and thus vulnerable. It has involved some shared knowledge, but it also has been a powerful experience for me. Knowledge is power—sometimes it brings hurt, but it also is essential for love and support.

This whole thing works because God is, and always has been involved, in community. The very nature of God, the Father, Son, and Holy Ghost, is God in community. Jesus set the mode of community in his relationship with the twelve apostles. Jesus said that where two or three are gathered in his name, he was in the midst of them. He believed in the importance of community.

The more we come to know Jesus, the greater impact he has on our lives. Like the Samaritan woman at the well, once we meet Jesus, we can't help being affected. Just as she grew in her understanding of Jesus, first as a man, then as a prophet, then ultimately as Messiah, we will grow in our understanding of Jesus as we get to know him better.

How do we grow in our knowledge of Jesus? My relationship is deepened when I spend time praying and talking with him. Watching Jesus work in the lives of fellow believers and in their ministry affirms the power of the Christ today in this world. Repeatedly, I have found it to be true that participation in a small group dedicated to Bible study, to spiritual growth in Christ, and to an in-depth relationship among its members is one of the most effective ways to grow in our knowledge of Jesus Christ.

Sure, there are risks in small groups. Christians fail one another too. But for me, the risk of some pain is outweighed by the joy of getting to know myself and my Lord in a deeper, more meaningful way. If indeed knowledge is power, I want as much knowledge of my Lord as I can get. And I want to share, to experience, this journey in the company of my friends.

As I would invite my independent friend, so I would invite you to start on this journey. In a world where all of us can be shaken, where we can be blown off course or lose our balance when we try to make it on our own, this kind of knowledge is absolutely the best power you could find anywhere.

# 19

# HE WAS MY AGE, AND HE WAS DYING

## STAYING INVOLVED THROUGH THE PAIN

*Martha said to Jesus, "Lord, if you had been here, my brother would not have died. But even now I know that God will give you whatever you ask of him." Jesus said to her, "Your brother will rise again." Martha said to him, "I know that he will rise again in the resurrection on the last day." Jesus said to her, "I am the resurrection and the life. Those who believe in me, though they die, will live, and everyone who lives and believes in me will never die."*

John 11:21-26

He was my age—and he was dying. Actually, he was maybe six or seven years older; but somewhere between graduation and retirement, the years merge into generations, the same generation experiencing the same things at roughly the same time. As men who had gone through much together, we had become friends.

He was my age—and he was dying. We were not only friends. We also had lived relatively similar lives. Both of us had worked long hours, he as a doctor, me as a lawyer; both of us had been married many years, in first and only marriages; and each of us had become the father of three children. I suppose that in many ways, we both were very grateful for all that had happened. But now there was one thing more.

He was my age—and he was dying. It was not the first time I

had come face to face with the reality of death. I remember, at around age five or six, traveling with my mother to a small Arkansas town to look one last time at the withered shell of her once overpowering father. He was dying of cancer; within a week he would be gone. I was the youngest grandchild of the youngest child who had survived to adulthood. He had fathered twelve and had seen nine grow to become big enough to leave the nest and live lives of their own. He was old, and he was dying. I remember picking flowers for him; I even remember the smell of the sickroom. It might have been because I was too young to understand completely, or it might have been simply because my mother was so stoic about it all; but the truth of the matter is that I don't really remember his death as a tragic event. He was old. It was the end. And, in true southern tradition, family feast followed family funeral, creating an almost festive atmosphere. However, death is still a grim matter for a child. No matter how easy it seemed to face, it left an atmosphere of imbalance among us all.

Mom died when I was fifteen—my second experience with death. It too shook my sense of a balanced life. Mother's death happened so fast. She took her own life. One moment she was saying good-bye and good luck, as I left for a student council campaign meeting. The next moment, we were at the hospital. A doctor with a serious face; an aunt in tears; and I in shock, with no feeling. It did not seem to be real, not for a long time. Yet she was my mom, and she was gone. It was a death too intensely felt to be real. And the circumstances made it seem unnatural. Thus it did nothing to prepare me for this friend's death; for he was my age, and he was dying. Each time I visited, I could not help identifying with him in some way.

Others had died before. Friends were killed in car wrecks from time to time, and there were acquaintances who had died someplace far away. They had been about my age, but somehow the suddenness, or the physical distance from the events themselves, seemed to insulate me from much identification. I guess I just did not see those deaths as precursors of my own.

But he was geographically near. He was here, and he was

about my age, middle age. Before I realized it, I had inadvertently become a participant in his death. I followed each step closely: chemotherapy, lost hair, good days, bad days, progress, relapse, hospital stays. All through that, the cancer had kept to its relentless course. Perhaps because he was my age and we had shared so much, for the first time in my life, the reality of the inevitability of my own death hit me hard. I can almost hear the slap, even now. That could have been me lying there! It *will* be me someday, maybe tomorrow, maybe in five, fifteen, twenty-five years. Death—"Remember that you are dust and unto dust you shall return." When it hits you in this way, it sets you spinning.

And he died. The usual forces had been mobilized—prayer teams, healing services, cheerful friends, the best available care. But he died. At the gathering of family and friends for his funeral, we sang, "I am the resurrection and the life. He who believes in me will never die." And I, despite the pain and dislocation of this particular loss, believed it. I would see my friend again. But I had felt the cold draft of a strange wind, despite my faith, and I had been shaken down deep inside.

What are we to do when we are slapped with the reality of the illness and death of a friend? I now realize the importance of accepting, in the relative calm of the good times, the reality of sickness and death. It isn't easy. There is something so final when it happens in my own life, in my circle of friends and family. Everyone agrees that, theoretically, we should accept that death is natural, just as life is natural. Yes, it makes good sense. But that almost seems too easy. Down inside, death still feels as if it were an intrusion. Even if it were at home in bed at the age 108, of "natural causes," there is something that doesn't feel right about it.

Ironically, our feeling of imbalance may relate to our common struggle with death's threat. We have a war against every disease. Every food is scrutinized. If we cut down on fat, we could save millions from death by heart disease. If we stay out of the sun or ban cigarettes, millions more will be saved from death by cancer. Somewhere, there seems to be the assumption that we may almost achieve immortality here on earth. But this is simply not true. All of us will die of something. Even the mention of Alzheimer's disease sends shivers down our spines. Saved from a heart attack at sixty to die of Alzheimer's at seventy? Which is a more natural death? It remains an enemy, as Paul called it, an intrusion into our lives. Ironically, we, the healthiest, longest-lived society in the history of humankind, seem to have the most fear of sickness and death, to focus on it much of the time.

But even if we accept that sickness and death are natural, what should we do when someone is sick, is dying? This is what I am exploring now, trying to regain my own sense of balance about death. I am exploring this out of the crisis I encountered when this friend, who was about my own age, died.

First, whenever you hear that a friend is seriously ill, stop whatever you are doing and start praying. Prayer became the primary foundation for me when my friend lay dying. And I don't mean just formal prayer. I mean a talking prayer, a tell-God-everything-you-feel prayer. And I discovered, in a new way, that I could actually tell that God was there. He was listening. He understood. Tell him you are afraid, that it could have been you. Tell him it isn't fair. Tell him you don't understand. The key is to tell him the truth. Ask him what you should do. Pray for healing for your friend. Pray for strength for you and your friend, and your friend's family. Pray for the right words to say, for the right actions to take. Pray each day, as often as you can, in the seconds and minutes you have; keep your dialog with God open. I actually did this. And in the mystery of prayer that never was answered *as I wished*, I came to know that God was deeply involved.

Second, don't desert your friend and your friend's family. Sickness and death are not at all pleasant. They scare people. We don't enjoy being around people in pain. Sometimes we are afraid we will say the wrong thing. Maybe we think they need to be left alone, don't want intruders at this time. We have hundreds of excuses to avoid the pain of being involved. Don't listen to any of your own excuses. Reject them. Go see your friend when you can, as often as you can, and whenever your friend is able. Hold your friend's hand. If you can't think of the right words to express your sentiments, buy cards and send them. Written words have a permanence that helps. Stay in touch. Be there—not just for your friend, but for your friend's family.

Third, when you are with your friend, don't ignore the subject of the sickness. I found that often our best times occurred when we talked openly about it. Sometimes when we are with a sick person, we want to act as if nothing has happened. This is actually so false that your visit becomes meaningless. If your friend is dying, this fact is real, and ignoring it will not make it go away. However, here is what worked for me. I let my friend be the guide. When he wanted to discuss his illness and treatment, I let him. I gradually learned to listen more carefully. I learned that he didn't need to hear stories about others' problems. I discovered that I needed to be sensitive to the fact that what he was experiencing was his illness, and it was very personal. It was truly unique—different from my own or others' war stories.

Fourth—and this may seem to be the toughest to do—when you leave your friend, in person or on the phone, say, "Would you like me to pray with you?" Or if you already have a prayerful relationship, by all means say, "Let's pray together." Simple words, yet often hard for us to say. If you have to, get tough with yourself about it. Fight the fear that might make you afraid to offer to pray with another. Our Western culture has the audacity to make us ashamed or timid about this. Don't push, but if your friend says yes, take his hand or hug his shoulder, and pray a simple short prayer such as:

> God, John is my friend. I love him. I know he is your child, and you love him too. Father, be with John in this sickness. We pray for health and healing. Give him the strength and courage to keep going in this fight. Give him the peace of the knowledge of your everlasting love. Amen.

The words are not as important as the acknowledgment of God in our lives and faith in times of trial. If you do this, you'll never forget it. Neither will he. And, I have come to believe, neither will God.

Fifth, always, always ask, "What can I do for you or your family?" And don't stop asking, even if the first few times he says he does not need anything. Ask anyway. Repeatedly. Just knowing that you care can be blessing in itself. And there may be a pressing need on a next visit that he is reluctant to broach unless asked.

Sixth, be there for his family. Include his wife and kids with your family whenever it is appropriate to invite them over or go someplace together. Don't let initial rejections keep you from asking again and again—not pushing, just being there. And if he dies, when he dies, turn your attention to his family, treat them as you would want someone to treat your loved ones if you died. Don't forget them afterward.

Finally, a big lesson we need to learn from this is that we cannot destroy the pain. The pain must be experienced. It has its own life; it is part of being human. It can't be denied, but it can be shared. It is an essential part of what it means to be human. Shoulders to cry on, hands to hold, handkerchiefs to dry eyes, quiet times just being together—this is how pain is conquered, not avoided.

Those are seven ways in which I have tried to regain balance for myself and for my friend at the time of his death. I'm still working with them. I am still aware that because we were the same age and had so much in common, we somehow shared his death together. Now that I am in my forties, I find myself reading the obituaries more often. "So and so died of a heart attack; age 42; survived by his loving wife and 3 kids . . . ." But this is not as threatening as it once was. I have discovered that death, this unnatural intruder, has become the special occasion when victory is closer than I had ever known it to be, when fear often has been met and overcome by love.

# 20

# WHEN A FRIEND IS HURTING
## BEING A FRIEND IN DIFFICULT TIMES

*Bear one another's burdens, and in this way you will fulfill the law of Christ. . . . So then, whenever we have an opportunity, let us work for the good of all, and especially for those of the family of faith.*

Galatians 6:2, 10

A friend of mine had been married for several years. He was a private person. We shared many interests and goals, but he never really talked about his family life. Seeing him over the years with his wife and kids, I never suspected there were major problems.

His pronouncement, "We're getting a divorce," struck me with a thud. But there it was, like an elephant in the middle of the room—too big to be ignored.

"It's so lonely," he told me. "No one has called. No one has included me, even for lunch. It's like I don't exist—never existed. Maybe I should have tried harder at developing close friends, but still, can't people see I'm hurting?"

Another friend lost his job when the company he was working for went out of business. The underlying fear of so many of us, in our all too competitive world, had become a reality for him. He was unprepared to deal with the grief that followed, grief much like that of a divorce or the death of a loved one. Suddenly everything changed. He no longer went to the office where he had gone every morning for years; he no longer saw the same familiar faces each day. He later confessed to me that one of the most difficult things to overcome was the blow to his self-esteem.

He told me, "You know, what has really surprised me is how difficult it has been to accept that I no longer work for a prestigious company, that some people treat me differently now. It is as if, in their opinion, I do not have the same value as before—or am not as competent." He came to realize that losing a job can be one of the most devastating losses for a man, because how we see ourselves as men is so tied to our work.

Still another friend thought he had everything in place. All his life he had worked hard and had achieved his dreams. He had a beautiful wife and two fine children, a nice house, a good job, a church family, and many friends. Then one day financial trouble hit, and everything seemed to come tumbling down around him.

In one way or another, all of us experience loss and pain in life. Why is it, then, that we often don't know what to do or say when friends are hurting? Sometimes it seems that our friends' hurts have a way of shaking our own sense of well-being and balance—even if we've "been there" ourselves and have made it through the pain.

So what are we to do? What does it mean to be a friend in difficult times? Sometimes simply being there brings more comfort and support than anything we can say or do. Friendship means being willing to stand beside a grieving friend's side. Even through the hardest times, being there to listen—to really listen, without judging or trying to solve the problem—is what being a friend is all about. Just listening to his vented frustrations can do wonders for a friend.

After listening, then what? I've found this to be good advice about giving advice: Do so only when your friend asks for it, and do so with honesty and Christian compassion. It may be that in light of the particular situation, you feel more comfortable consoling, comforting, or reassuring, rather than giving any so-called advice. Remember that your role as a friend is special and unique; it is not the same as that of a minister or counselor, though you might suggest that your friend talk to one. And chances are that your friend does not want you to play those roles; he wants you to be his friend.

So what do you do after listening and offering whatever support, encouragement, and help you can? Simply this: pray. Pray for your friend, his family, and his particular situation. Pray that he will have courage, strength, and wisdom. Pray that you will be a good friend and know what to say and do. Pray on your own and with your friend, putting your faith in the power of prayer.

Once, in the middle of a dark time in my life, I didn't think I could go on. I was praying to God to let the crisis pass. And then it hit me. I realized the reality of Christ for me—the Christ in Gethsemane, on his knees, saying, "Let this cup pass." Christ knew anguish and despair, but he also knew the power of prayer.

At different times in our lives, different images of Christ rise up in front of our eyes—Christ the healer, the feeder, the miracle worker, the gentle teacher, the cross sufferer, the risen Savior. But in my darkest hour, the Gethsemane Christ reminded me that nothing, not even death, can separate me from the love of God. And nothing I will ever face can compare to the agony of my Savior and the reality of his sacrifice for me, a sinner.

After that experience, I started praying and reading the Bible every day, and I became involved in small groups with other Christians. I drew strength from this fellowship. As I heard others share their own faith stories—how God and Christian friends had helped them through illnesses, money problems, divorce, the death of loved ones and friends, and even imprisonment—I realized that all of us are broken people, healing in Christ.

The problem of loss is one of the most disturbing questions in our lives. It will be among the greatest challenges we or our friends will ever face. Like Job, we will never be able to make sense of the bad times or tie them up with a ribbon. But like Job, we can hold on to our faith and affirm that God is always with us. As you grow closer to God in your own journey through life, you will find in this relationship not only the strength to recover from loss, but also the grace to be of inestimable help to your friends.

May we always bear one another's burdens.

# 21

## ONE TRUE LOVE

### OVERCOMING THE MYTH OF THE "PERFECT" MATE

*A capable wife who can find?*
*She is far more precious than jewels.*

Proverbs 31:10

I just know that somewhere out there, there is one special person just for me, one true love, and when I find her, I will know she is the one."

Our culture, where marriages are often based on romantic love, relies heavily upon what I call the myth of the one true love. According to this viewpoint, marriage is the union of two people who are destined for each other. Unfortunately, these high expectations often result in dissatisfaction. They can actually lead to unhappiness, even divorce, when the romanticized fantasies are not realized.

Several years ago I attended a marriage seminar at my church. The leader talked about a study that involved hundreds of couples who had been surveyed to find how they felt about their marriages after one year, five years, and ten years. The survey used a rating system of zero to 100, with 100 being tremendous and zero being the pits. The results of the survey caught me by surprise. It was totally opposite from what I expected. Those who rated their marriage, after one year, at 90 or above, on the high end, or at 40 or below, on the low end, had divorced after 5 or 10 years. Those who rated their marriage at 60 to 90 were still married, and still rated their marriage between 60 and 90. Most of those who rated their marriage between 40 and 60 had sought marriage counseling; some were still married, and some were divorced.

The seminar leader concluded that those who had rated their marriage above 90 had totally unrealistic expectations as to what marriage was all about. Therefore, when those expectations were not met, when the reality set in after a few years, they divorced. Those who rated their marriage, even in the first year, at less than 40 had serious relationship problems and could not hold it together. Those who rated their marriage at 60 to 90 had much more realistic expectations of marriage and were able to make the compromises that made it work.

This study was significant, the leader told us, because it supports the idea that a score of 60 was likely to indicate a good marriage. It meant that you had to accept that 4 out of 10 experiences in marriage might not be so hot. But it all depended on how you looked at it. His point was that we can choose how we dwell on that 60 or that 40 percent in our own marriage. If we focus on the 4 bad elements, we won't feel good about the marriage, even though 6 aspects of it are good.

There is a danger with this approach, of course, because we should not spend too much time trying to reduce our marriages to some form of matrimonial bookkeeping exercise—judging and evaluating every little thing. It sounds too egocentric, self-indulgent. A healthier, more balanced approach is to follow the advice a wise, long-married friend once gave me. He said, "When it comes to problems in marriage, don't sweat the small stuff. In reality, if you actually compare whatever is bothering you to the value of sustaining your marriage, you will discover that it is almost always small stuff!" My friend was really saying that commitment, communication, and compromise are powerful tools for working out the problems we all face in our marriages. I like this approach, but it does shoot a big hole in the myth of the perfect spouse, the perfect marriage.

This may give an initial sense of balance about your marriage, but keep it in perspective. Nothing this side of heaven is perfect, but balance also can be so steady and motionless that it becomes boring. You must have at least some daily vibrations in that balance to keep from falling asleep. Here are three fitness tips for vibrancy in that balance.

1. Eat supper together each day. Don't include your greatest rival—the TV.
2. Show how much you value what the other is doing each day, whether at home or at work. Don't just ask, "How was your day?" or "What did you do today?" Anybody could do that. Get involved. Pursue with questions of how it felt, what it meant, what was left out, and so forth.
3. Be physically present. Some of us are the all-or-nothing types. I am not talking about sex. I am talking about the remaining 99 percent of the physical opportunities: Take her hand, walk together, sit beside each other. Contrary to the good ole boy myth, if you haven't discovered it already, women are physical.

Marriages that exhibit all three of these characteristics just don't seem to have problems. Marriages where at least two of these attributes are present are not only balanced, but also in motion. But when only one or none of these is present, the marriage is headed for problems. It may be balanced, but is nearly dead still.

So you say this is unrealistic. You're on the road. You can't be there for supper all the time. I have been there too. My work schedule and my travels often keep me from making it to the supper table. So arrange special times together, dinners or mini-vacations, even if just for one night. Your own personal one-night stand with your own wife! Sound crazy? It can be a marriage saver. Remember the goal: Balance with motion, with life.

This sense of balance can come in a variety of ways. In his book *I Was Just Wondering,* Philip Yancey includes a chapter called "The Spirit of Arranged Marriages." He discusses the difference between marriage in the West, where the lovers choose each other, and the East, where the families often arrange the marriage. Yancey notes that one reason there is less divorce in the East is that the parties bring an entirely different perspective into the marriage. It's decidedly more pragmatic. Rather than seeing the spouse as the fulfillment of a search for the one true love, they see their husband or wife as a partner. And they see their marriage as a union that they must make work. Thus, they focus on achieving the goal of a successful marriage. Love, one hopes, grows into the marriage as part of the achievement of this important goal. The marriage isn't based on the host of unrealistic expectations about romantic love that we have in the West. The partners are free to focus on what can be done to make the union work—the combination of balance and motion.

My experience of living in a culture where there are many people with arranged marriages has verified Yancey's insight. I have a friend who is an accountant with a big company in Asia. He is about my age and has been married about as long. He has three kids, just like I do. But here is the difference: He had met his wife only once before they were married. What's more, they had spoken for only about fifteen minutes. A recipe for failure, right? I found it very hard to accept that someone could agree to spend his whole life with someone he did not even know.

"Marriage isn't like that with us," my Christian Indian friend told me. "Marriage is a union of two families. My family and hers, in a large extended family. We have to take care of each other. We have to accept the duties that come with life. As the oldest son, I must be sure that my mother is always taken care of after my father dies. In addition, I must be sure that my sisters are properly married. These are duties I cannot ignore. It is also part of my duty to marry, to bring children into the world, and to take care of them. I really can't imagine a life where all I need to think about is myself and what I want."

Well, nobody arranges our marriages here. Our weddings, yes, but not our marriages. Can't imagine it. But I must admit that in many ways, my Indian friend seemed to have a more mature attitude about marriage and the duties that come with it. Here is the bottom line: The elements of duty and responsibility are the building blocks of the love. We've been doing it backward. If you have tried to build your marriage out of a search for fulfillment and self-actualization, you know what I mean. You end up way out of balance. What has happened is that we have fostered a climate where too often, when the going gets tough in a marriage, the not so tough among us get out.

Did you see the movie about the man who is celebrating his fortieth birthday? His father has died recently, and he now has the burden of taking care of his overly dependent mother. To compound the matter, his teenage son is in a lot of trouble and needs his dad to help him. Still more, his middle-aged wife, becoming insecure about her own physical attractiveness, is trying harder than ever to be sexy. He feels strangled by all the ties, the responsibilities of his life.

So what does he do? He buys a Porsche, starts dating a Dallas Cowboys cheerleader, separates from his wife, and tries to run away from all his responsibilities. For a while, it seems to be working—great experiences, moments of ecstasy. His dreams are coming true. No responsibilities.

Then one night he shows up at his girl friend's door, unannounced. She refuses to let him in, and he sees another man in the room. When he starts to become angry, she reminds him that they had agreed, no strings.

He realizes that he really does not want this "freedom." Without commitment and responsibility, it really equates to loneliness and isolation. He realizes his life had meaning only when he had those. He needs strings! Here is where forgiveness enters the picture and he learns about love. His wife takes him back. He is able to resume his life.

Many men go down the path he took and are not so lucky. We forget that commitment is conducive to love, not vice versa.

Your marriage may already be out of balance, swinging too far to one side, about to crash. Or it may be locked into place. Either way, it's not in balance.

Here is what you can do. Keep it in perspective. Sixty percent may be better than 100 percent. Try the three marital-fitness steps for thirty days. *Really try.* No cheating. And pray for your wife every day. Being in balance is like a dance—you have to be flexible, adaptable, and open to positive change.

Keep this in mind: Commitment, duty, and responsibility are the building blocks of love. They are the foundation stones for your marriage. Nothing else works. More than that, however, they will help you put out of your mind forever the myth of a one, true, perfect love. Get rid of that myth, and your marriage has a chance to become strong enough to withstand whatever life throws your way.

# 22

# My Friend Peter Pan
## CHOOSING COMMITMENT

*Once Samson went down to Timnah, and at Timnah he saw a
Philistine woman. Then he came up, and told his father and
mother, "I saw a Philistine woman at Timnah; now get her for
me as my wife." But his father and mother said to him, "Is
there not a woman among your kin, or among all our people,
that you must go to take a wife from the uncircumcised
Philistines?" But Samson said to his father, "Get her for me,
because she pleases me."*

Judges 14:1-3

I don't think I will ever marry again," my friend mused one
day after a run together. My friend was forty. He had been married once, in his early twenties. He and his wife had no children.
After a few years they had grown apart, and since then he had
led the single life. He had been through a series of jobs and relationships. Handsome, intelligent, athletic, and witty, he never
had trouble finding a date. He was in a current relationship; I
knew the woman. She was beautiful, smart, committed to her
career, and, like him, divorced with no kids. He lived in a lake-
view condo filled with modern furniture. He gave every appearance of living the "good life," taking frequent vacations and
beach trips. He had few responsibilities, plenty of money, a challenging job—and, at forty, he was still "young."

"It's not that I don't want to remarry," he continued. "It's just
that, well, I know the pattern. I meet a terrific woman. We hit it
off. We start to date. Everything is dynamite. But after a time,

it's just not the same. The excitement fades. I begin to see the flaws and, well, it just dies. About that time, I usually meet another terrific woman who seems to be all I want and need, and the pattern repeats itself." Like Samson, my friend seemed to be using the wrong measuring stick—his own pleasure.

He continued, "At first I hope that maybe, just maybe, this time it will work. Breaking up is hard, but truthfully, it gets easier with time. I know I will get over it, and with the excitement of a new relationship, it's easy to forget the breakup. And yet, there is always this underlying sense of melancholy that is hard to shake. I have this nagging feeling that time is passing quickly, and my chances are limited. Each time I start dating another woman, I ask myself, 'How long will it last this time? Why can't I have a lasting relationship?' "

As I listened, I thought of Peter Pan. You know the story: He refused to grow up. Psychologists talk about the "Peter Pan Complex," the restless desire to keep moving, to avoid a lasting commitment, to keep all options open. I did not try to answer his question. Instead, I simply listened. I felt him yearning to achieve something that had been beyond his reach.

I thought how different our lives are. I, too, married young, but I am still married. My wife and I have three kids. Our marriage isn't fireworks all the time, but would I want anything else? No. Would I give up the depth of my ties for the insecurity of one of my friend's new relationships? No. So what is the difference between me and my friend? I wondered. It was as if he were trying desperately to maintain a "balance" in his life: so much work, so much fun, so much solitude, so many relationships, so many friends, and so forth. Yet balance seemed to elude him.

Not long ago, a news magazine featured a cover article on the chemistry of romantic love. The article identified a specific chemical change that takes place when we fall head over heels in love—the love-at-first-sight phenomenon. It went on to say that scientists have pinpointed certain natural chemicals that are released in our bodies when we "fall in love." These chemicals have an amazing effect on us; they bring a powerful sense of euphoria. In fact, they provide the same sense of "rush" that comes with the use of certain drugs; and over a period of time, we can almost become addicted to experiencing that "rush." But in time, the impact of these chemicals fades—no matter how exciting someone may have been at first. After a while, we no longer have the same strong chemical reaction to the person that we once did.

The author refers to the familiar example of caffeine. Suppose you normally drink two cups of coffee a day. Gradually, those two cups of coffee will lose their effect on you; you'll begin to want three. Over time, you will require more and more coffee to produce the same sense of satisfaction. Here is the comparable problem: It is actually possible to become overdependent on the feeling of romantic love. Just as with cups of coffee, it gradually takes more romantic love to achieve the same effect.

The article speculated that these chemical reactions occur in humans to encourage mating and reproduction, just as they do in other animal species. In other words, romantic love is basically a chemical reaction, preprogrammed by our instincts. The author attributed the breakdown of many relationships to the loss of this chemical reaction. When the reaction stops and romance faces, many people long for a new chemical "high." Thinking they are no longer "in love," they often search for a new love.

Though there may be some truth to this, people are more than a series of chemical reactions. That was exactly my friend's problem. He had plenty of chemical reactions, but deep in his heart, he ached. Pleasure, work, and material things were not enough. Something was missing. His life was still out of balance.

I have another "Peter Pan" friend who is five years younger than I. When we first met, I was in my late twenties, the epitome of stability—a wife, one child, a house, and all the trappings of middle America. He was single, as were most of his friends. He lived in an apartment, drove an old car, and paid cash for everything. He refused even to own a credit card. He loved his freedom. He and his older business partner had been clients of mine, and at first, our relationship was simply business.

Then one night, when I was thirty-two and he was twenty-seven, I was working late. I decided to get something to eat and walked from my office to a new restaurant that was popular with the younger crowd. My family was out of town, and I planned to eat a quick dinner and return to the office for a few more hours. At the restaurant, I ran into this friend and some of his single friends.

When he saw me, he teased, "Hey, Martin, what are you doing here? You're an old married man. Thirty-two is too old for this place. You better sit with us so you don't stick out like a sore thumb!" I was a little embarrassed, but I did join them, and for the first time, this friend and I began to talk on a more personal level.

After that, we begin to exercise together and talk about our lives. For me, his eyes were a window into the single world I did not know—had never really known. I learned that, in many ways, his world was much less complicated than mine—by his conscious choice. He didn't feel that he was ready for the responsibilities of a wife, kids, or even a house. He valued his freedom. He was constantly on the move, meeting new people and starting new relationships.

My life was so different. I had married while still a student, settled into a profession, started a family, bought my first house, and become active in church. I had begun to accumulate the "strings," the ties that bound me to my wife and kids and community. The lessons I was learning Sunday after Sunday and in the small Bible study groups I was attending were challenging me, pushing me forward. Life was changing for me at present, but in a far different, more profound way. I was finding a sense of balance.

My friend, on the other hand, seemed to be frozen in time, locked into a lifestyle that was incredibly self-focused but lacked commitment to anyone—no strings. His life may have appeared balanced to some, but it wasn't. Sometimes "balance" can be deceptive, and he knew it; but he was not ready to change, to accept the challenge of commitment.

When my friend turned thirty-two, I called him and asked,

"Hey, where did you go on your birthday?" He answered that he and some friends had gone to that same restaurant where we had been a few years before.

"What?" I said. "Thirty-two is too old for that place!"

He laughed and said, "Okay, you got me. Go ahead and twist the knife." What surprised me about my friend was that at thirty-two, he was no different from the way he had been at twenty-seven. He was doing the same things, stuck in the same place in life.

A few years later my friend began to change. I could sense his restlessness, his desire for more meaning in his life. We went to several church-sponsored men's retreats together, and my friend started praying more and more, seeking a stronger relationship with God. He also began to look for someone to build a life with—a wife. I believe there is a time and a season for everything; my friend's time for settling down simply came later in life than it did for me. One day he called to tell me he was getting married. He had found the right woman; the time was right.

Now my friend is happily married and has a son, a home, a demanding job, and all the "strings" that he used to tease me about a decade ago when he was "free." And guess what? He would not trade those strings for all the "freedom" of his youthful days. What made the difference? I believe it was the renewal of his relationship with God that opened his eyes and led him to become a man of commitment. This is the life we are called to as men, as husbands, and as fathers. There are no roles more important for us to play.

Each of us knows at least one Peter Pan, someone who can't bring himself to confront the deeper issues of faith and commitment—the kind of commitment necessary for a lasting, fulfilling marriage. Despite the hopes and dreams of these Peter Pan friends, good chemistry won't last forever. Alone, it results in an unbalanced equation.

As my second Peter Pan friend discovered, each of us must make three important choices if we are to leave the Peter Pan of adolescence behind and become men: (1) the choice to be honest with ourselves and with God; (2) the choice to accept the fact that growth and contentment come from commitment, rather than from "having it all" or seeking personal pleasure; and (3) the choice to give of ourselves to others, to care more about the well-being of others than about ourselves. These are not easy choices for those who are stuck in the "Peter Pan Complex"—nor for any of us, who are basically self-centered human beings. But with God's help, they are possible to make and to keep. And they produce remarkable results!

# 23

# THE POWER OF AN IMPERFECT LIFE

## LETTING GO OF "HAPPILY EVER AFTER" EXPECTATIONS

*He called the crowd with his disciples, and said to them, "If any want to become my followers, let them deny themselves and take up their cross and follow me. For those who want to save their life will lose it, and those who lose their life for my sake, and for the sake of the gospel, will save it."*

Mark 8:34-35

Do you remember the movie titled *The Cutting Edge?* In that film, a blue-collar Olympic hockey player, who is injured and cannot become a pro, is hired to be the partner of a temperamental, artistocratic Olympic figure skater who has gone through several other partners. This unlikely duo fight, fall in love, win the gold medal, and, presumably, live happily ever after. Our hearts are warmed—life is good—happiness reigns supreme. Only it doesn't always work that way, does it?

We expect, almost demand those lived happily ever after endings. Many people were angry when Margaret Mitchell refused to rewrite the ending of *Gone with the Wind* so that Scarlett would be reunited with Rhett instead of returning alone to Tara. We really aren't comfortable with less than "happily ever after" endings. When Barbara Streisand and Robert Redford made their famous movie, *The Way We Were*, they left many fans gasping. It was so bittersweet: two people from totally different backgrounds fall in love, but it doesn't work out. They don't live happily ever after. Ouch. Perhaps it reminds us of something that we know deep down is true.

One Christmas before Kay and I were married, I gave her a music box that played the theme song from *The Way We Were*. It was not a smart move, for the hauntingly beautiful melody evidently carried a message just the opposite of what I intended. I remember that Kay got the strangest look on her face when she opened that present. Both of us were more committed to the "happily ever after" idea than I had realized. It wasn't until a few months later, after we were engaged, that she confided that when I gave her the music box, she was afraid I was trying to tell her good-bye—that we were not going to make it, just like the lovers in the song.

That music-box incident occurred more than nineteen years ago. It comes to mind again because Kay and I have found that life never is perfect, that we continue to do things that are far less than perfect. Certainly there has been much joy in our marriage, including the blessing of three wonderful children. However, we also have made many mistakes and carried many burdens. We have had peaceful moments, but we also have had some very serious struggles. Yet the truth is that our marriage is stronger because of what we have worked through together. I have come to accept that we won't live "happily ever after"—tomorrow, the next day, or from here on out. You won't, either. What I also have come to know, however, is that as Christians, we can live through the unique power of an imperfect life.

Here I must admit something. Sometimes we Christians promise more than God actually provides. Let me explain. We can inadvertently create the expectation that life with Christ can usher in a life of living happily ever after—all problems solved, peaceful times ahead. The only problem is that it isn't true. Surely, the message of reconciliation with God, forgiveness of sins, unconditional love is exhilarating. When we understand and accept that Jesus died for us as sinners in our brokenness, and that nothing we do can separate us from the love of God if we will admit our sin, repent, and accept God's grace, we feel the burden of sin slip away. The only problem is that the burden of life remains.

In *No Wonder They Call Him the Savior,* Max Lucado tells the story of a poor South American woman who is trying to raise her daughter alone in a small rural town. The daughter grows up bright and beautiful. She longs for so much more than the rural life she sees ahead of her. And so, at age sixteen, she runs away to the city. Her mother knows that there is only one way her daughter can earn a living in the city—prostitution. The mother sells all she has, goes to a photo booth, and makes pictures until the money runs out. She writes a note on the back of each picture and places them on bulletin boards in seedy hotels and restrooms, hoping that her daughter will see one of them. When all the pictures are gone, she goes home to wait.

A few weeks later, the daughter, hardened and more worldly now, sees her mother's picture on the bulletin board of the broken-down hotel where she has been working. She picks up the picture, turns it over, and reads:

> Whatever you have done,
> Whatever you have become,
> I love you.
> Come home.

The daughter returns home. A great story, right? And undeniably a profound truth. Yes, Jesus loves me. Yes, I can always come home, no matter what I have done or who I have become. And yet, as I reread the story, I can hear the faint echo of "and she lived happily ever after." In reality, it isn't so. Let's face it. It must have been extremely difficult to return to the village, to her mother, to rumors and condemnation from neighbors, to the reality of a lost dream and a shattered life. Loved? Yes. Forgiven? Yes. Accepted back into the home with her mother? Yes. But happily ever after? No way. The burden of sin may slip away, but the burden of living an imperfect life in an imperfect world may actually be felt all the more.

As Christians, we believe that a relationship with Jesus Christ changes us inside and that this transformation of character begins to change other things as well. When we walk with Jesus Christ, it affects every aspect of our lives.

Even so, Christianity is not an insurance policy against problems. The early church followers certainly were not spared the burdens of carrying Jesus' cross. Imprisonment, beatings, and even death were the rewards for lives dedicated to Christ. I also think about the lives of the persecuted Christians in the former communist countries behind the Iron Curtain who suffered for so many years because they refused to renounce their faith.

So why should it be different for us? Often our mistake is that we have such blessings that we sometimes equate the "good life," the "perfect life," with God's blessings for his faithful people. But when bad things happen, when the "happily ever after" begins to get a little rough around the edges, we tend to blame ourselves or God for the things in life that we cannot change.

A friend of mine told me how angry he was at God. He wanted to find someone to love, a woman he could marry. He wanted a family—the "perfect life" as he imagined it. He had prayed to God, and yet each relationship would fail. Why? Why wouldn't God answer his prayers? Implicit in this railing against God was the assumption that because he was trying to lead a good life, to trust in God, God should give him a wife. I am also sure that he harbored the idea that the right woman, the right relationship, would lead to the scenario of a wonderful marriage, and they would live happily ever after.

I didn't have an honest answer for him; I have been there myself, about other things in life. I knew that simply telling him that Abraham had to wait many long years for God's promised Son would not make this man feel any better. I wanted to say, hey, we're not guaranteed wives, money, health, friends, and so on just because we believe in God or try to do good. God doesn't deal in guarantees. He deals in calls to his service to take up the cross, to suffer for his sake, and to endure the toils and trials of this life by discovering the balance and power of an imperfect life that is lived under the lordship of Christ. Even the person who is miraculously cured of cancer will die one day of something. People we love will become sick or die in our lifetime. We will mourn and grieve. Heartache and tragedy are a natural part of living in this broken world.

Yet there is good news, as Paul told the Romans: "I consider that the sufferings of this present time are not worth comparing with the glory about to be revealed to us" (Rom. 8:18). Paul understood pain, but he grasped something deeper than pain itself. He was assured of God's glory.

We too can be assured that our faith in Christ will sustain us until we can be with him. In the meantime, we must stop trying to discover whether there is more joy than pain in our lives. That is a search for the "happily ever after" ending, which will never come in this world. Instead, we need only rejoice, as Paul also said, that our names are written in heaven, and God's glory will cover us.

Modern life has become so cheap and shallow that we are tempted to settle for the superficial answer, the oversold pronouncement. Paul gives us depth, the assurance of grace in the midst of imperfection, in the midst of pain. In a world that talks about power, that depth is the real key to power.

# 24

# THE PECULIAR CONTENTMENT OF THE CHRISTIAN LIFE

## FINDING REAL JOY

*Sing praises to the LORD, O you his faithful ones.*

Psalm 30:4

As I was driving to work, I stopped alongside another car at a traffic light. It was a sight to behold! There was a sweet, white-haired, grandmotherly lady in an old Ford Escort, just singing away: "Under the boardwalk, down by the sea, Yeah . . . ." She had such a look of joy on her face, as if she hadn't a care in the world. Compare that scene with the one I had seen earlier, just before I dropped my older son off at school. An angry, designer-dressed, fur-coated woman in a late model Mercedes convertible had blown by me on a narrow residential street. I do not know where she was going in such a hurry or what pressure was tormenting her. Nevertheless, all morning the pictures of those two women haunted me. And, oddly, the question that drove me was, "Which one of them was more content?"

Perhaps I already had begun to ask that question of myself, because in my quiet time that morning I had looked through some illustrations of the book of Ecclesiastes. The author of this edition had chosen a picture to depict each of the verses in this great book. As I gazed at the illustrations of the joy, pain, despair, wealth, poverty, and all the other states of humankind reflected in these pages, I was overwhelmed with the truth of this profound Old Testament book. There are times and seasons of life, and who can explain them?

Contentment is perhaps one of the most intriguing ideas, for it is the attitude that helps us to endure almost any hardship, any tragedy that comes our way. On the other hand, the idea of happiness seems such a fleeting, ephemeral thing. No one really knows what it is. Happiness seems to be dependent upon a sense of pleasure, however subtle. On the other hand, contentment is a state of being that goes far beyond the difficulties of the moment. It includes a profound sense of balance. So many people have suffered things I cannot begin to fathom, with the contentment of their hope for a better life hereafter and a thankfulness for what they have today.

Our minister just returned from a leave of absence in which he and his wife visited a poor African country. He told a remarkable story about a fund-raiser held at a local church, where the congregation was trying to retire a debt of $3,000 for a new parsonage. The parsonage had no electricity, plumbing, running water, indoor bathroom, gas, or any of the things that would be minimally required in this country to avoid a structure being condemned. Even so, they were quite proud of it. So the parishioners held an auction. After each of the elders had publicly declared how much he would give, each member did the same. They clapped for one another as the money was dropped into the plate.

Then they started auctioning off the things that each had brought: eggs, sugar, wheat, and other basic necessities. One man brought a stem of bananas. Another remarked that he would never bring bananas because they cause constipation. Everyone laughed, and then two sides began a bidding war for the bananas. The bananas brought the highest price at the auction. When one side finally won, all the people on the winning side pitched in to help the man who had placed the bid, because, of course, he did not have that much money. Then he gave the bananas to the man who had made the remark about constipation. Everyone laughed and was full of joy.

Then the elder pulled out the last of his money. As he put it in the plate, he said it was his "widow's mite." The rest of the people dug deep one more time and contributed again. In the end, it was announced that they had raised more than $50. Everyone cheered wildly and rejoiced at their good fortune. The minister remarked that he was amazed that these people with so little could exude such joy, such contentment. Their books didn't balance, but somehow their lives did.

Have you ever wanted to be content? Would that mean the end of desire? I know it is not as simple as just being poor and therefore appreciative of small things. Neither is it simply a matter of having money. It has something to do with a deeper part of our lives. The problem is that poverty, starvation, sickness, and lack of medical care are always with us; they create real suffering.

There is a saying that goes something like this: "I have been poor and miserable, and I have been rich and miserable, and I would rather be rich and miserable." Well, given that limited choice, who wouldn't? Nevertheless, the whole point of Ecclesiastes—and, I believe, of the message of Christ—is that we are not called to be limited by these alternatives. Here is the catch: Contentment means different things to different people. We in the "blessed" West often equate contentment with material possessions or a comfortable lifestyle. And we have a harder time finding true contentment, true joy, because our material possessions clutter up our lives. We are preoccupied with worry about losing them and envy for what others have.

The Eastern religions posit that they hold the answer to contentment by teaching people to rise above the world and its pain, or to turn within themselves to a place where the world cannot touch them. Their solution is to reach the point at which one is no longer able to feel pain.

Wherever we may live in this world, the case is really the same. It won't make much difference whether you drive a Ford or a Mercedes. Neither will retreating from the world and its problems. Contentment is entirely an internal matter—an internal matter with external results. As Christians, we are called to seek contentment through discipleship, love, prayer, and the commitment to do something about the pain and problems of this world.

There are two ways to seek contentment and expect something new to happen in your life. One way is to practice a serious commitment to the spiritual discipline of Bible reading and prayer. It will bring definite and dramatic results. However, you must be willing to make it a regular—even a daily—practice. The second way is to give a significant amount of time each week to service to others.

The fullness of life includes both joy and sorrow. In the final analysis, contentment is embedded in the deep confidence that, ultimately, God will resolve all the contradictions of life. It is not simply, as Ecclesiastes puts it, the balancing of a time to laugh with a time to cry, within the limits of this world's horizons. It is balancing, both now and later, the cross and the Resurrection, the beginning of salvation and the end. We learn this only as we grow stronger through the commitment to Bible study and prayer, and the selfless giving of ourselves to others. This is the peculiar contentment of the Christian life. It will balance many areas of your life. It may even enable you to break out singing "Under the Boardwalk" more often, to the surprise of everyone, just because it feels good.

# 25

# IS MY LIFE TOO COMPLICATED?

## OFFERING YOUR LIFE AS A GIFT TO GOD

*[W]hat does the LORD require of you*
*but to do justice, and to love kindness,*
*and to walk humbly with your God?*

Micah 6:8*b*

Sometimes we feel that our lives are too complicated, our jobs and our responsibilities too demanding or too unusual for us ever to achieve a true sense of balance. However, an experience I had several years ago made me realize that there is hope for any of us.

I had gone on a personal retreat to the Abbey at St. Gregory's College in Shawnee, Oklahoma. My sister had taken courses there, had told the abbot about me, and I had been invited to come. I needed a retreat: It was a time of struggle in my life, a time of questioning. Father Philip, the abbot, had been kind and encouraging on the phone; I'm not sure what I intended to discover there about myself, but I knew I needed something.

As I settled into the unusual routine, I could feel a rhythm about the place that was almost hypnotic. The cycle of daily prayers, the regular mealtimes, the discipline and surrender to the way of the monastic life—all this contrasted dramatically with the "ordinary" world in which most of us live, the crazy demands that continually come at us. From the moment I walked through the door, I knew that this was going to be a different ball game.

The monk's path was clear. Here I knew where I would be and what I would be doing at morning prayer, at breakfast, at noon prayer, at lunch, at evening prayer, at dinner, and so forth. I was told when I was to be silent and when I could speak. Rules about everything, even more than in the army. There was no introduction, no explanation, no justification offered: obedience was all.

Yet there was a peacefulness in the simplicity of this world. And, oddly enough, it turned out to be too brief a visit. I had specialized in making choices, facing up to the demands of a hectic life. I had come to feel that I was burdened by responsibilities. But as I soaked in the Benedictine way and savored the respite, I wondered if it would be possible to incorporate something from this experience into my daily life on the outside.

Of all the things I saw and experienced on the retreat, what stayed with me was the unique sense of balance I saw present in the lives of the monks. As I had never been in a monastery before, I had no idea what the monks would be like. I suppose I simply thought that they might be somewhat like Friar Tuck, or maybe the scholarly Thomas Merton. I really never considered meeting someone like Brother Kevin.

Brother Kevin was the Abbey's mechanic. He laughed as he told me that he had been a monk there for thirty-five years, and he guessed he would stay there until he died. He had even picked out where he would rest in peace in the Abbey cemetery. This man possessed one of the gentlest spirits I have ever been around. His tanned face, warm smile, and childlike eyes belied his years. His voice was soft and melodious. His hands, rough and permanently stained with the oil of all the college and Abbey machinery he lovingly maintained in his shop, gave a firm shake as he introduced himself.

Earlier, we had exchanged a few words over lunch, the one meal during which the rule of silence was lifted. He asked simple questions: Where was I from? What did I think of the college? There was a genuine curiosity behind each question. I did not sense any hidden agendas, ulterior motives, or attempts at judgment—matters that we so often become aware of in our daily lives in the secular world.

Later that evening while walking, I met him at the flagpole. We talked as I walked and he rode his bike around the campus. I mentioned the beautiful grounds, and he told me how different it had been when he had attended St. Gregory's as a boarding student and then as a college student. He had never left, staying on to become a brother. This was the life he was called to, he said. He could not imagine any other. The brothers were his family. This life was his response to his understanding of God's plan for him. He seemed so at peace with himself, with this simple life. He was, from our ordinary perspective, a simple man. He had no desire or ambition to become a priest or to move up the ladder in the church hierarchy. He had no need for possessions. He just wanted to work with his hands and worship his God in the community with his fellow monks.

Brother Kevin also told me that his journal writing took the form of letters to many people with whom he corresponded. Because he was not a teacher at the college, I did not think his letters would be to former students. As a mechanic who had lived the past thirty-five years in this cloistered environment, I could not imagine who his correspondents were. Just as I was about to ask such a question, a car pulled up and two young men got out.

The first, a good-looking fellow who appeared to be about twenty-one, walked up to Brother Kevin, gave him a big hug, and said, "Brother Kevin, I want you to meet my step-brother." I could not hear all their conversation, but I believe that the former student was explaining that his step-brother would be attending college there the next year and needed to know Brother Kevin.

I introduced myself, and Brother Kevin explained that this young man used to come around to the shop and help him. They had become good friends. I wondered how many young men, over the decades, had been influenced in this way by the cheerful gentleness of Brother Kevin. No doubt some of them are the continuing beneficiaries of his example and receive his letters.

And Brother Kevin gave something to me. His gift was simply a reminder of how little God really asks of us. Balance comes to us in strange ways. Sometimes we get caught up in the thought that we can find the good life or serve God only through some grand accomplishment or supreme sacrifice. The truth of the matter is that my conventional approach to the well-balanced life had run out of gas. Certainly, part of the force that drove me to the monastery in the first place had been a struggle with the question of how I could really serve God and still deal with the daily grind of making a living and being there for my family. I know I had been wondering how I could keep it all balanced, how I could really love and serve God with my whole heart, mind, and soul.

At the other end of the spectrum, I wondered whether Brother Kevin's life was too unusual. Had it become unbalanced in other ways? His simple life appeared to me to be a total gift to God. Each activity glorified his Maker. The key lay not so much in his way of life as in his dedication. His contentment, which showed so clearly in his words and visage and actions, is a rare thing in our circles today.

As I left Brother Kevin, deep in conversation with his old friend and the new student, the words of the prophet Micah echoed in my head: "And what does the LORD require of you but to do justice, and to love kindness, and to walk humbly with your God?"

One gift I received from the Abbey was the realization that I needed to view my whole life in a different perspective. I needed to see even my struggles as a service, as a gift to God. Brother Kevin could do it, and I could do it. I realized that lifestyle isn't the issue. Of course, some lifestyles aren't acceptable. You can't offer cheating your customers to God. Likewise, you can't offer cheating on your wife or ignoring your children to God. But you can offer to God anything that is good and honest, whether successful or not.

The Monday after I returned from the Abbey, I discovered

that a client had not chosen me for an important project. This client used many law firms and could choose from many people who were qualified for the work. Nevertheless, I was deeply disappointed. Who wouldn't be? So I started to follow an old pattern for dealing with disappointment. I thought about going home, eating a bag of Oreo cookies, and commiserating with Kay about how unfair the world is—wallowing in the familiar mud of self-pity and martyrdom. OK, I could do that. But would that restore any balance to my world? I then remembered Brother Kevin and the your-life-can-be-a-gift-to-God attitude that I had experienced just the day before. This would take some doing.

I decided to go for a run around Town Lake. As I ran, I talked to God. I told him about my disappointment. I said that this time I was not going to stuff myself with sweets to cover the bitterness of disappointment. Instead, I would just experience the pain and offer it up to him. When I got home that evening, I felt better. Everything wasn't resolved, but I was headed for a new sense of equilibrium, of balance in my life. Kay and I then talked long into the night. Something was beginning to change inside.

I would *like* to say that since that day, I have approached every disappointment, each painful event in my life, with the same resolve to hand it over to God. But it would not be true. This takes more effort than I had first thought. Mother Teresa and Brother Kevin are far easier to admire than to emulate. But I am on the path. I've learned that I can't blame my problems on the kind of job I have or the responsibilities and pressures in my life. It's my attitude that makes the difference. I have found that it helps to focus directly on Jesus. With Jesus as my friend, I can begin to feel a closeness to God. By sacrificing for my friend, just as I sacrifice for the other loved ones in the my life, I begin to experience a deeper sense of love, mature love. I know I have only begun this journey. But what I have learned is this: No matter how complicated or simple, how ordinary or unusual our lives may be, we can offer them as a gift to God.

# EPILOGUE

I once took my children to the circus. One of the acts was a clown spinning plates on wooden sticks. He started by spinning one plate on one stick, and he kept adding sticks and plates until he was spinning ten plates on ten sticks. Talk about a struggle for balance! And yet he made it look simple and fun. As I watched, I noticed that he was very deliberate in his well-practiced actions. He had a plan; he knew where he was going and what he had to do to get there. And he succeeded. I decided there were lessons I could learn from his performance. Many of these lessons can be found in the pages of this book.

In a world where there is much that would keep us out of balance, we do have a choice. As impossible as it sometimes seems, you and I can experience a greater sense of balance than ever before. I have tried to explore some of the important questions and share some choices and changes that work—that result in more balanced, faithful living. There is much that each of us can do, but we must have a plan. Like the clown at the circus, we must know where we want to go and how we plan to get there. We must move deliberately. We must practice, try, fail, and try again. But with God's help, we *can* make a dramatic difference and experience the joy of God's balance in our lives.

# Questions for Reflection or Discussion

## 1. Why Not the Best?

1. What does the concept of doing your "best" mean to you? Do you think doing your best is something you should strive for? If so, why and under what circumstances would there ever be a time when you should try not to do your best?

2. Has there ever been a time in your life when you felt that you had done your best? If so, how did you feel? Why did you try so hard to do your best? Did you succeed in what you were trying to accomplish?

3. Have you ever experienced failure while trying to do your best? What did you learn from that experience? Can you remember a time when you consciously did not do your best? How did you feel? What was the result? What lesson did you learn?

4. Do you ask yourself what others will think before you buy something, go somewhere, or do something? If so, do you think this concern is good? Are there times when you *should* consider the opinions of others before you act? If so, when, and whose opinions?

## 2. Too Large a Pizza Pan and Too Little Dough!

1. On a scale of 1 to 10, rate the priority of the following areas of your life, according to the amount of time you give to

each: work; family; church; friends; community; self—mental; self—physical. Do you think this test is a fair reflection of these areas' true importance to you? Should something other than time be the primary measuring rod used to determine the priority of these areas?

2. Do you believe that the allocation of time among competing priorities should be influenced by your stage of life? Are there, or should there be, different priorities for the single man, the young married, the married with children, the middle-aged with grown children, the retired? If so, in what ways might they differ?

3. Do you have short- and long-term goals for your life? If so, do you consult them when making decisions about allocating your time? If not, why? Have you communicated these goals to your family and those who are important to you in achieving these goals? Do you periodically reevaluate these goals, in light of your progress and current priorities?

## 3. Crossroads

1. Think about important decisions you have made in your life. How did you make those decisions? What impact have those decisions had on your life?

2. Have you ever made a crossroad decision and later felt that you made the wrong decision? If so, why? What were the consequences? What lessons did you learn from that experience?

3. What areas of your life are most vulnerable to making the wrong crossroad decision? What steps can you take to make the right decisions in these areas?

4. To whom can you turn for help in making good decisions? Who knows you well enough to ask you about the areas of your life in which your weaknesses could get you into trouble? What can you do to develop this kind of accountable relationship, if you do not have it now?

## 4. Why Go to Church?

1. Do you go to church regularly? Why, or why not?

2. What was, or would be, important to you when deciding which church to attend? What do you consider the most important result of becoming part of a church?

3. What church activities and ministries do you participate in, and why?

4. Is Sunday a special day for you and your family? Do you take one day a week and make it holy? Do you rest one day a week? Should you?

## 5. What Separates the Men from the Boys?

1. Think for a minute or two about recent advertising you have seen or heard. What sort of picture does it paint of the man who would purchase that service or product? Is that picture appealing? Why, or why not?

2. How has your sense of what it means to be a man changed or remained the same through the years?

3. Do you sense God calling you to change or refine a way of talking, a thought pattern, or a particular behavior? If so, list these things. Then, under each one, list some straightforward, practical ways you may be able to answer his call.

## 6. I'm Only Human . . . ?

1. When was the last time you excused some action by saying or thinking, "I'm only human"? What did you do, if anything? How did you decide to take that action? If you had the chance to do it over again, what would you do differently?

2. Have you ever tried to imagine what Jesus would do when faced with a choice like one you were facing at a particular time? If so, what happened? If not, how might your actions

have been different if you had asked yourself this question before you acted?

3. What changes can you make in your life today to bring your actions more in line with what someone created in the image of God should be doing?

## 7. On Our Own Special Course Through Time

1. Are you comfortable with the person you are now, at this time in your life? How important to you is your physical appearance?

2. Do you now enjoy life more or less than in the past? Do you think tomorrow will be better? Why, or why not?

3. What, if anything, would you change about your past? How has your past made you the person you have become?

4. What are you doing, or what can you do today, to make tomorrow better? Try to picture yourself in five, ten, fifteen, and twenty years; then describe who you will be, what you will look like, what your interests will be, and how you will be living your life.

5. How will the decisions you make about your future affect the futures of those you care about? How much should you consider their needs and desires when making decisions that affect your future?

## 8. How Deep Is Your Rudder?

1. Recall a time in your life when you made a decision that had negative consequences for you, your family, or your work. What were the circumstances that led to the decision? What could you have done differently?

2. How do you determine what is right and wrong in a given situation? Whom or what source do you consult, if you have questions about what the best decisions would be?

3. Have you written a personal mission statement to articulate who you are, what kind of relationship you want with your family, how you want to conduct yourself in your job, and what you see as your responsibilities to your church and community? If not, set aside an afternoon in a quiet place where you can be alone and think. Prayerfully write your mission statement. If you already have a mission statement, does it still reflect how you see yourself, and where you want to be in life? What changes should you make?

4. What can you do today to deepen your rudder? Do you belong to a small group of fellow believers who meet regularly, study the Bible, and support one another? Do you keep a journal? Can you find thirty minutes, ten minutes, or even five minutes a day to pray, talk to God, and read his Word? How do you think this might change your life?

## 9. Have You Put God in a Box?

1. Have there ever been times when you thought you knew exactly what God wanted and later found out that you were wrong? Do you think you can disagree with a fellow Christian about God's will, and both of you be right?

2. Have you ever prayed specifically about your work? If so, what kinds of prayers have you offered, and how has God responded? If not, what career concerns or issues do you need to share with God in prayer?

3. In what ways do you incorporate God in your workday? How do you know what God wants to happen in your life and job?

4. Compose a prayer to God, asking him to be Lord of all your life, including your work. Or write a letter to God about how you view your work. Reread the letter and ask yourself what changes you need to make in your life, if any.

## 10. Does God Care About My Work?

1. Think of examples of sacrifice and work in the Bible, such as the parable of the talents. How do you think God views work?

2. Can you think of others who were or are willing to make great sacrifices in their work and lives for the sake of others? What do you think about the value of what they did or are doing?

3. What sacrifices have you had to make in your life? For whom, and why? How do you feel about those sacrifices and the effect they have had on you, and on those for whom you sacrificed?

## 11. The Myth of the Perfect Job

1. How and why did you choose your current job? Do you enjoy what you do? Why, or why not? Do you see yourself in this same job in five years, ten years, until retirement?

2. What do you expect from your job? How would you describe the perfect job? What can you do in your present job to make it seem more like the perfect job?

3. What do you think you owe your employer, if you are not self-employed? What relationship do you see between your faith and your obligations in your job? What do you think God expects of you in your job?

4. If you do not like your current job, what can you do to determine whether you should change jobs? What should you do while you are considering all the options? Is there any value in accepting the frustrations of your current job?

## 12. Daily Bread

1. Do you think a person can be a Christian and drive a BMW? Why, or why not?

2. How do you make decisions about how you spend money? What role does your Christian faith play in these decisions?

3. How important to your happiness are money and the things money can buy? How much do you worry about the future and your financial security? Are your priorities and concerns in line with God's plan of Christian stewardship?

4. How do you use what God has given you to help others? Is there anything you need to give up or change in your life, in order to shift your focus from your needs to those of others?

## 13. What Do Men Live By?

1. How would you answer the three questions posed to the angel: What is given to men? What is not given to men? What do men live by? Can you think of examples from your own life that support your answers?

2. Has there ever been a time in your life when you were faced with a decision like the one that faced the good Samaritan? How did you respond? How do you think you might respond in the future, if faced with a similar situation? What would determine when you would become involved?

3. How do your actions and your decisions about material things influence your children's (or loved ones') attitude about money and wealth? What lessons are you teaching them? What can you do to encourage good stewardship in your children (or loved ones)?

4. Rate yourself on your generosity. If you died today and faced God, what do you think God would say about how you treated his creatures? Beginning today, what can you do to be more like the righteous in the passage from Matthew 25?

## 14. What Will They Say About Me When I'm Gone?

1. Who are the "Aunt Myrtles" in your life? Whom do you admire, and why?

2. What are the character traits that you would like others to see in your life?

3. If someone were to write your eulogy today, how would it read?

4. Write a eulogy that you would like to reflect your life. What steps can you take today to bring your actions more in line with the life you want to lead?

## 15. Whose Life Am I Living?

1. How much have your parents influenced the decisions you have made in your life—your interests, your friends, your jobs, your spouse? Is parental approval more or less important to you now?

2. What accomplishments are you most proud of in your life? Why?

3. How do the attitudes of your family, friends, and co-workers influence the decisions you make about where you live, the kind of car you drive, the clothes you wear, and so forth? What role does God play in the choices you make?

4. In what ways can others see God in your life?

## 16. My Dad Is a Workaholic

1. If you have children, write down how each one might describe you, using language appropriate to the child's age. (This won't work unless you honestly try to imagine what he or she *really* thinks.) If you don't know, make an "appointment" with each child to have lunch or supper and find out. Even if you do know, make that appointment and talk with your child about a typical workday for you. Encourage your child to tell you about his or her "work," too.

2. Think of a time when work responsibilities caused you to disappoint your family. In what ways did they make their

disappointment known? How did you feel? How did you respond? If something similar happened again, what might you do differently?

3. What would you like to change about the balance between your work life and your home life? Why? What difference would this change make? Or if the balance is about right, how did you achieve it?

4. What would it mean to put God and your family first in your life? What would this require of you at times when a conflict between work and family cannot be avoided?

## 17. My Father, My Friend

1. How would you describe your father? What are his values? What motivates him? How would he describe himself? How might his description differ from yours?

2. In what ways are you like your father? What character traits do you share? What values do you hold in common? How are you different?

3. What do you think your father was like as a child? As a man your age? How has your own growth through the stages of life influenced your relationship with your father?

4. Is your father your friend? Why, or why not? What can you do to improve your relationship with your father?

5. If you have children, do they think of you as a friend? Do you want them to? Why, or why not? What can you do to help your children develop and become comfortable with their own gifts, desires, and interests?

## 18. Knowledge Is Power

1. Think of your closest friend. What do you like about that person? How did this friendship develop? How do you sustain this friendship?

2. Do you have any friends who share a commitment to growing in your relationship with Jesus Christ? If so, in what ways do you do this? If not, how might you cultivate such friendships?

3. Describe the attributes you want in a friend. Then describe yourself as you think your friends see you. Imagine one of your close friends telling a stranger about you. What would he say? Which of the desired attributes you named do you need to work on?

## 19. He Was My Age, and He Was Dying

1. Has anyone died to whom you were really close? How did you feel? How did you react? What would you do differently today, if the same set of circumstances occurred?

2. What are your fears related to sickness and death? What promises of the Christian faith give you hope?

3. How would you want your family and friends to respond, if you were diagnosed with a fatal disease? How do you respond to others who are suffering and in need of a friend?

4. If the doctor told you that you had only four months to live, how would your life change? Which of these changes should you implement now, in order to begin living more fully today?

## 20. When a Friend Is Hurting

1. Think about an occasion when you were having a difficult time in your life. Was there a special friend or friends who helped you through that time? What did they do? When have you been that kind of friend to others?

2. What makes someone a good friend? What does it mean to "be there" for a friend?

3. Think of a recent conversation with a friend. Did you spend more time listening, or talking? Was the conversation on a superficial, or more personal level? What things are you uncomfortable or unwilling to discuss with friends? How can you give support and encouragement when you or your friends experience problems in any of these areas?

4. When, and in what ways, do you pray for your friends? Do you ever pray with friends? Why, or why not? How has prayer—whether private or shared—been of help in a particular situation?

## 21. One True Love

1. Do you believe in "love at first sight"? Do you believe that there is only one person with whom you are destined to spend your life? How have the answers to these two questions affected your relationships?

2. Think of a couple, friends or family members, who have had a long and successful marriage. Do they seem particularly well suited to each other? Are they happy all the time? How do they relate to each other and handle conflict? What can you learn from their example?

3. If you are married, what would your percentage rating be on the satisfaction scale from 0 to 100? Why? Has your opinion changed much since your first year of marriage? How, and why? Would you approach your marriage differently, if there were no such thing as divorce? How?

4. Imagine that you lived in a culture where your wife was chosen for you by parents, and you did not know her before you married. What would you do to try to make the marriage succeed? What attitudes and expectations would you bring to the relationship? Can you incorporate any of these ideas into your existing relationship?

## 22. My Friend Peter Pan

1. Do you have a "Peter Pan" friend? How about yourself? Do you see any of these tendencies in your life?

2. Think for a moment about how you have changed in the last five, ten, and fifteen years. Do you see little change? Do you see growth? Why? What do you hope you will be like in five or ten years? What can you do to make this happen?

3. Do you agree or disagree with the article's findings about the chemical processes involved in love? Why?

4. Describe, in your own words, what love means to you. What is the difference between romantic love and committed or unconditional love?

5. How would you define commitment? How important is commitment to a successful relationship—particularly a marriage relationship?

## 23. The Power of an Imperfect Life

1. As a Christian, how do you reconcile your faith and God's promised blessings with the disappointments in your life?

2. Do you believe that God intervenes in your life and the lives of others? How? In what ways? Why do you pray? What role does prayer have in God's relationship to you and your life?

3. What do you think heaven will be like? What do you really believe about the promise of paradise and resurrection? How does this belief affect the way you live your life today?

## 24. The Peculiar Contentment of the Christian Life

1. Who are the happiest people you know? What sets them apart from others? What do you think makes them so happy?

2. How content are you in your daily life? Why? What can you do to improve your level of contentment? What can you do about those things over which you have no control or cannot change?

3. Is there a difference between being content and being happy? If so, what is it? Have there been times in your life when you were content, but not happy? What enabled you to be content?

4. List the things that bring you real joy. How often do you do or enjoy these things? Can you incorporate more of these into your life? Why, or why not? When can you start?

## 25. Is My Life Too Complicated?

1. When was the last time you felt a need to simplify your life? (*That* recently?) What did you do about it? Make a list of realistic things that could simplify your life—the list may be as long as you like. Now choose one or two achievable things, and ask God to help you accomplish them.

2. Think of someone you've met who seems to possess true serenity. Do you have any clues as to why this is so? If so, are any of these things applicable to your own life?

3. Try to recall a time when you experienced great inner peace (in childhood or adulthood). What were the circumstances? Describe them in detail, out loud or on paper. Can any of these circumstances be duplicated in your present life, if only for an hour or two a week?

4. As an experiment, the next time you have a disappointment or rejection, try to imagine putting that experience on some great stone altar in a rugged outdoor spot, and then setting it afire, as a sacrifice to God.